Core Skills In English

English

3

Grammar
Comprehension
Creative writing

Teacher's Notes

This book aims to introduce pupils to the salient features of English grammar. The books develop pupil's ability to comprehend written passages and utilise both grammar and comprehension in a series of relevant and structured exercises. The passages have been carefully chosen to give a wide variety of interesting material drawn from both fact and fiction.

How the books are constructed

Comprehension

The extracts of writing are of varying length and sentence construction. Each passage is followed by a dictionary exercise based upon words found in the passage and a series of questions. In some cases the answers are explicit in the passage while in others they are implicit. Some questions go beyond the confines of the passage and draw on the pupil's more general experience and skills.

Grammar

The points of grammar introduced are those which will enhance the pupil's style of writing and speech. Grammar is not treated as an end in itself; technical names for parts of speech, for example, are only introduced where they are useful. Each point is introduced by a brief explanation and followed by several sets of reinforcement and consolidation exercises.

Written style

In each book there are several sections that aim to broaden and develop the pupil's written style. These vary from drawing attention to over-used words and suggesting alternatives to extending sentence construction.

How to Use these books.

Each book contains more work than you are likely to need in one school year. Therefore you will probably need to be selective. This may be achieved in a number of ways. You may decide to concentrate on one particular aspect of the book, say grammar or style, and use the other parts incidentally. Alternatively, you might decide that it is not necessary for the pupils to complete every exercise — that the appropriate skill or point will be better developed with extended teaching time and reduced time on the exercises.

The comprehension passages, in particular, lend themselves to a number of differing approaches. They can certainly be used by the individual child but they can also be used by groups of children, thus providing the basis for useful discussion. They could also be used as completely oral exercises. By starting with some of the shorter passages you could provide a progressive course in listening skills.

Whatever you decide to do, you will find that this series, as well as providing a core scheme, will enable you, the teacher, to achieve a high degree of flexibility of approach.

ISBN 1 85276 0230

© Scholarstown Educational Publishers Ltd., London. 1988.
Printed by Folens Ltd., Dublin.

Contents

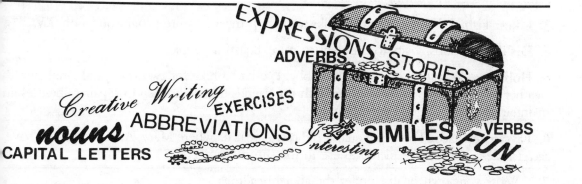

EXPRESSIONS
ADVERBS STORIES
Creative Writing EXERCISES
nouns ABBREVIATIONS Interesting SIMILES VERBS
CAPITAL LETTERS FUN

Profile

Read the following profile which Nora Lawless has written about herself.

1. Facts

Name	Age	Birthday	Address
Nora Lawless	Eleven	5th June	The Granary, Gorebri Midlothian EH23 4FQ

Height	Weight	Hair	Eyes
1m. 57cms	40 kgs.	Brown	Green

Brothers	Sisters	Uncles	Aunts
2	None	6	3

School	Class Teacher	Principal	Pupils
Gorebridge	Mr. Robson	Mrs. Atkinson	123

2. Friends: My two best friends are Mary Mayers and Ann Rodgers. Mary is tall and dark, wit brown eyes and curly hair. Ann is small and fair, with straight hair. We play every day and o Saturdays we go swimming in the local pool.

3. Likes: Fish and chips, country walks, cats, pop music, nature programmes on T.V.

4. Dislikes: Onions, visits to the dentist, mice, boastful people.

5. Hobbies: Cycling is my favourite hobby. I've had a bike for two years and whenever th weather is fine I cycle in the country with my friends. I have learned to repair punctures an maintain my bike in good condition.

6. Favourite Place: There is a quaint old castle near us where Mary, Ann and myself have secret hide-out. We have picnics there in the summertime.

7. Write your own profile under the above headings.

Capital Letters

Capital letters are used for:

(a)	The start of a sentence.	**Example:** My father works very hard.
(b)	The names of week-days, months and festivals.	The school is open from Monday to Friday. Every country celebrates Christmas Day.
(c)	The names of people, a title when used with a name, titles of relations when used with **actual names**.	Mary Jones is my friend. She shook hands with President Hillery. He met his Aunt Mary in town.

(A) **Insert the capital letters where necessary in the following sentences.**

1. last thursday, the school closed and remained closed until monday.
2. joan smith and michael murphy are cousins.
3. good friday and shrove tuesday are two important days.
4. mary and john casey are my friends in school.
5. the president met bob geldof.
6. the duke of albany was a very rich man.
7. april the first is 'fools' day.
8. we saw our uncle tom's new car.
9. the lecture was given by professor kelly.

Capital letters are used for:

(a)	"I" when used on its own.	I do not know why I failed my exam.
(b)	The names of places and words made from the names of places.	Dublin and Cork are two cities in Ireland. Not all Frenchmen speak French. Some speak Breton.
(c)	Titles of books, films, plays. (Quotation marks are necessary.)	Louis Stevenson wrote "Treasure Island".

(B) **Insert the capital letters where necessary in the following sentences.**

1. i ran until i thought i would collapse from exhaustion.
2. Thousands of lancashire and yorkshire supporters travelled to Wembley to see the game.
3. Shakespeare wrote the play "julius caesar".
4. Everybody knows that dublin is a large city in ireland.
5. We import oranges from valencia in spain.
6. We went to see the film "jaws".
7. The river mersey flows into the sea at liverpool.
8. i would like to read "huckleberry finn" a second time.
9. The plane flew from london to paris and then on to rome.

The Gold Mine
Comprehension

Gold fever is a catching disease, and even a ten year old was not *immune*. One warm June day, when I was on my way to join my father, I came on an abandoned mine. The ladders, still in place, seemed sturdy enough, and curiosity led me to go down the shaft alone, something I was strictly forbidden to do.

The mine was fairly shallow, and when I found a candle stub on a ledge and matches in a corked bottle, I decided to explore. I had visions of finding a wonderful overlooked gold *deposit*. Ten metres in, the tunnel forked briefly into a Y, but in each branch, I found only unrewarding granite walls.

I had blown out the candle and replaced it on its ledge, and was preparing to *ascend* the ladder when I felt it tremble in my hands. Someone was coming down! In a moment I heard voices. There were two men. Panic squeezed my chest; they must be the owners of the mine, and they were about to catch me red-handed trying to steal their gold.

I ran back into the tunnel and *groped* my way along the left branch of the Y. Soon they, too, entered the tunnel. They wore candle-lit miners' hats, and one of them carried a shotgun. With all my strength I pressed against the back of the tunnel, and only when they entered the right branch did I let out my breath. Suddenly there was a loud explosion, then a second one.

I suspected almost immediately what the men were doing. Father had often talked about the various methods of "salting" a mine in order to sell it to some *unwary* buyer. Sometimes the tricksters brought in rocks containing gold ore and *strewed* them around the tunnels. Sometimes, as in this case, they loaded shotgun shells with gold and fired both barrels into the mine walls.

Dictionary work: Find out the meaning of these words and write each one in a sentence of your own: immune, deposit, ascend, grope, unwary, strew.

Questions:

1. Why, in your opinion, was the mine abandoned?
2. Give two reasons why the child was forbidden to go alone into abandoned mines.
3. Write out the sentence which shows that the writer's search for gold in the mine was unsuccessful.
4. Why were the matches kept in a corked bottle?
5. How did the child first learn:-
   (i) that more than one man was entering the mine?
   (ii) that one had a shotgun?
6. Why did the men not discover the child?
7. Whom were the men trying to trick?
8. Why did the men carry shotguns?
9. Write a suitable ending to the story.
10. Write a list of the precious stones and metals you know.

Opposites

(A) Write the opposite of the words in bold type.

1. The **private** house is situated near a **quiet** road.
2. Mary **purchased** a **big black** statue.
3. The **junior** partner in the firm **sold** the house.
4. The **innocent** man was punished by the **coward**.
5. The **small** rats **retreated** along the dusty road.
6. The **miserable** man **cried** when he **lost** his dog.
7. The **dwarf** lifted the **light** bar over his head.
8. The **proud** soldier waited for the train to **arrive**.
9. Joan has a **permanent** job in the **new** factory.
10. The **cheap** case fell on the **poor** man's toe.

(B) Find the missing words in the following sentences. The two words must be opposite in meaning.

Example: The apples were *juicy* but the figs were *dry*.

1. He .... a new bicycle and s .... his old one.
2. I borrowed a book from the pr .... library as the pub .... library was closed.
3. The oranges were pl .... but the prunes were sc ....
4. The cats ad .... along the street but when they saw the dogs they r ....
5. The ex .... of the building was not as beautiful as the in ....
6. The main en .... was guarded by police but I escaped through a side e ....
7. The timber was r .... but the plywood was s ....
8. He pleaded i .... in court but the jury found him g ....
9. He dived in at the d .... end of the pool and swam to the s .... end.
10. I was lucky to find a v .... space in the car park and I o .... it.

(C) Rewrite these sentences to give the opposite meaning.

1. The sea was very *calm* when the boat *left*.
2. The *old* man *walked slowly down the road*.
3. She *released* the *healthy* pigeon.
4. Every *morning* he watched the sun *rising in the East*.
5. He *bought* the *sweet* grapes at the *high* price.
6. They rowed *slowly* across the *deep* lake.
7. He *ascended* to the *top* of the mountain with great *difficulty*.
8. The *handsome* prince *found* the *bright new* key.

Addressing Envelopes

Dawn Gill
10 Oriel Close,
St. Albans,
Hertfordshire MK31 4JT

(i) The stamp is placed at the top right-hand corner. Do you know why?
(ii) Write the name and address in good clear writing.
(iii) The first line of the address should start well away from the top of the envelope and a little to the right.
(iv) Have each line in the address a little farther to the right than the previous one.
(v) A comma is placed at the end of each line except the last line.

Instead of 'Mister', write Mr. When writing to a woman, use Mrs., Miss or Ms.. A full stop must be placed after abbreviated words,
Examples: Co. meaning County
 Initials of people's names, A. meaning Anne.

(A) Write down what the following abbreviations mean.

Co. .... Rd. .... Ave. .... Sq. ....
St. .... Pk. .... Dr. .... Tce. ....
Cres. .... Gro. .... Cl. .... Upr. ....

(B) Write the name and address of a person you know on this envelope.

Note:
line 1 : name.
line 2 : street, road or townland.
line 3 : town.
line 4 : county and postcode.
line 5 : country (if letter is being sent abroad).

(C) Draw envelopes and address them, using abbreviations where necessary.

1. Miss Joan Moriarty, 17 Castle Avenue, Glossop, Derbyshire SK13 9BR.
2. John Reynolds, 88 Market Square, Bingley, West Yorkshire BD16 3EZ.
3. Mrs. Maria Burke, 116 Greenfield Road, Wythenshaw, Manchester M23 6RT.
4. Mr. Paul Ryan, 48 Brandon Park, Saltford, Avon BS18 3EN.

Jack, Knight of the Roads
Comprehension

Old Jack was on his last journey, and he knew it. A *racking* cough shook his withered frame that shivered under his tattered, *scanty* clothes. *Furrows* of pain dug themselves into his wrinkled, *pallid* face. He knew he should not have left his miserable lodgings, but he had no more money left to pay the nagging landlord.

Another few kilometres to the next village and a friendly house, food and a fire. What would he not give for the warmth of a cosy fire! It was bitterly cold. Jack had never before felt so exhausted and *famished* with the hunger. He was forced to rest at the summit of the hill. He could not have picked a more unsuitable place. There was neither rock nor hedge to shelter him, and the biting wind, like red-hot needles, pierced his poorly-clad body.

His *gnarled* fingers tightened their grip on the blackthorn stick. With despairing eyes he searched the wild and rugged countryside for the friendly shelter of a house. Nothing met his gaze save bare, ghost-like trees, *bleak* hill-tops and the cold greyness of frost-covered fields.

He groaned pitifully and with a last great effort he *summoned* all his courage and staggered forward. He had hardly moved a step when his strength failed him and he collapsed in a heap on the roadside.

Dictionary work: Find out the meaning of these words and write each one in a sentence of your own: rack, scanty, pallid, famished, gnarled, bleak, furrow, summoned.

Questions

1. "Old Jack was on his last journey and he knew it."
   What signs indicated to Jack that it was his last journey?
2. Why was the beggarman plodding along the countryside on such a cold day?
3. What words in the opening paragraph convey the picture of a poorly dressed man?
4. What characteristics of winter are emphasised in the third paragraph?
5. Why did Jack choose to rest near a bleak and desolate hill-top?
6. How does the author arouse the reader's sympathy for Jack?
7. Find words in the story which mean:-
   (a) exposed and barren
   (b) to suffer severely from hunger
   (c) finding fault incessantly
   (d) lacking in colour
   (e) shrivelled and shrunken
   (f) wearing ragged clothes
   (g) to be deprived of strength
   (h) twisted and knotted

Masculine and Feminine

(A) Write the feminine form of the words in bold print. *(Study page 95).*

1. The **actor** and the **poet** went to see the **mayor**.
2. The **duke** and the **prince** visited the king.
3. The **host** and **his servant** welcomed the **bridegroom**.
4. The **manager** and the **waiter** served the **man**.
5. The **bachelor** and **his brother** lived alone.
6. The **landlord** and **his grandson** travelled to London.
7. The **abbot** and the **priest** prayed together.
8. The **ram** was killed by a prowling **tiger**.
9. The wild **stallion** had a beautiful black **colt**.
10. The **drake** and the **gander** attacked the boy.

The drake and the gander attacked the boy.

(B) Write the masculine form of the words in bold print. *(Study page 95).*

1. The **headmistress** kept a **vixen** as a pet.
2. The **heiress** remained a **spinster** all **her** life.
3. The **countess** bought a **mare** for a thousand pounds.
4. The **nun** and the **mayoress** spoke at the meeting.
5. The **bride** and **her sister** discussed the arrangements.
6. The **authoress** wrote a novel about the **heroine**.
7. The **shepherdess** came upon a lost **nanny-goat**.
8. The **postwoman** spoke to my **niece**.
9. The **traitress** was brought before the **empress**.
10. The **witch** cast a spell on the **tailoress**.

(C) Write these sentences in the plural.

1. The actress starred in the film.
2. The boy would not write the letter.
3. The husband waited for his wife at the station.
4. The princess liked the play.
5. The king set out to hunt the wolf.
6. The lady drank a cup of tea.
7. The prophet speaks in the holy book.
8. The fox attacked the hen.
9. The goose followed the child down the road.
10. The fisherman hooked the trout.

The lady drank a cup of

Over-used Words

Said

Instead of the over-used word 'said', use some of the following words in the sentences below.

(jeered, asked, ordered, groaned, begged, grumbled, demanded, shouted, whispered, answered).

1. "The pain in my shoulder is getting worse," *said* John.
2. "Your bike is not as good as mine," *said* Joan.
3. "The teacher gives us too much homework," *said* Tim.
4. "Can you swim four lengths of the pool?" *said* Paul.
5. "I can easily swim four lengths," *said* Mary.
6. "There is to be no talking during fire-drill," *said* the teacher.
7. "Please bring us to the circus," *said* the children.
8. "I want my money back," *said* the customer.
9. "Don't make a sound or they will hear us," *said* Eileen.
10. "If you do not behave yourself. I will order you off," *said* the referee.

Lovely

The word 'lovely' tends to be over-used or used too loosely. Rewrite the following sentences, replacing 'lovely' with some of the words in the brackets.

(panoramic, interesting, delicious, pretty, daring, thrilling, talented, sunny, beautiful).

1. The *lovely* girl was wearing a *lovely* dress.
2. It was a *lovely* day so we prepared a *lovely* picnic.
3. The view from the mountain top is *lovely*.
4. The children listened to the *lovely* story.
5. He performs some *lovely* stunts in his latest film.
6. Everybody agrees that she is a *lovely* musician.
7. It is a *lovely* adventure tale set in the Amazon jungle.

Got, Get, Getting

Rewrite the following sentences replacing 'got' 'get' 'getting' with one of the words in the given list.

(lift, became, mounted, bought, plunged, preparing, escaping, boarded).

1. The outlaw *got on* his horse and succeeded in *getting* away.
2. I *got* a new football in town and *got on* the bus to Workington.
3. My brother *got* nervous while he was *getting ready* his speech.
4. *Get up* the rock and throw it away.
5. The diver *got* into the clear water.

Letter-writing

Read carefully the following letter.

Sea View Hotel,
7 High Street,
Tranmere,
Merseyside L13 4BD.
5th June 1988.

Dear Mam and Dad,

A thousand thanks for your welcome letter which I received this morning. I was excited when I saw it lying on the table. You have no idea how thrilled I was to receive the £5 note. It was as good as winning the National Lottery.

I am delighted to know that you are all well at home. Mary and I are having a wonderful time here in Tranmere. The weather is glorious, the people are kind and the food in this hotel is excellent. We are both as brown as berries and go swimming every day.

Tell Tom that I'll write to him tomorrow. Remind him to feed Bonzo regularly. I miss you all. Give my love to May and Declan.

Your loving son,
Karl.

Some rules and observations.

(i) The writer's full address must be shown at the top right-hand side of the page.

(ii) Each line of the address is a little to the right of the previous line, as shown.

(iii) Names of houses begin with capital letters but no quotation marks ("....") are required. Examples: St. Anthony's, Avondale, Elm Tree, Silver Meadow.

(iv) The date must be clearly indicated. You may write the date in a variety of ways. Examples: 3rd June, 1987. June 3rd, 1987. 3/6/1987. 3/6/'87.

(v) Begin: Dear Mother, Dear Sir, Dear Madam, Dear Mrs. O'Brien, etc.

(vi) End: Yours truly, Yours sincerely, Yours faithfully, Yours respectfully, Your fond friend, etc.

Exercises

1. Write out correctly the following letter.
   74 Worship St., Clerkewell, London EC2A 2EN. 5th June 1989.
   Dear Denise, Mary and myself are going camping to the Llyn Peninsula next month.
   We would love to have you come with us. Remember what fun and enjoyment we had in Cumbria last year? Do try and arrange your holidays so that you can come with us.
   Your fond friend, Olive.

2. Write a short letter to a friend, asking her or him to come on a day's outing with you.

3. You are camping with the scouts by the sea. Write a letter home to your parents.

4. Write a letter to your friend, inviting him or her to your birthday party.

Pioneers of Flight
Comprehension

An ancient Greek *legend* tells us of Daedalus who made a pair of wings and flew to freedom ⁕om the island of Crete where he had been imprisoned. He also made wings for his son, Icarus, ⁕t he was not so lucky. *Disregarding* his father's advice, Icarus flew so high that the sun melted ⁕e wax which held his feathers together, and he plunged to his doom. The legend may be ⁕true, but the wish to fly like the bird has been a constant *preoccupation* of humanity from the ⁕ginning. For hundreds, perhaps thousands of years, many brave experimenters tried ⁕successfully to imitate birds until it was finally realised in the eighteenth century that such a ⁕at was an impossibility. Attention then switched to lighter-than-air machines and ⁕periments began with hot air balloons. The *theory* was simple: hot air is lighter than cold air, ⁕ if a balloon is filled with hot air, it will float. To put the theory into practice was quite a ⁕fferent matter, however. The honour finally fell to two French inventors, the Montgolfier ⁕others who, on September 20th 1783, succeeded in putting the world's first aerial passengers ⁕oft in a balloon. The event took place at the palace at Versailles in the presence of Louis XVI ⁕d Marie Antoinette, and the "passengers" concerned were none other than a sheep, a cock ⁕d duck! This was a month before Francois de Rozier dared to sail in a balloon above Paris.

But the invention of the balloon did not satisfy the age old desire of mankind to fly. The ⁕lloon was a clumsy, *flimsy*, dangerous and unreliable structure which simply drifted wherever ⁕e wind happened to blow it. Another pair of brothers, Wilbur and Orville Wright, had set ⁕eir sights on constructing a heavier-than-air flying machine. What they came up with was a ⁕range-looking machine with engine, propellers, wings and *rudder*. The Wrights had built the ⁕rplane. On December 17th, 1903, Orville became the first person to achieve motorised flight ⁕hen he flew the machine for 12 seconds, covering a distance of 36 metres at Kitty Hawk in the ⁕S. Later that same morning, Wilbur flew for 59 seconds and covered a distance of 280 metres. ⁕ *revolution* in travel was about to begin.

⁕ictionary work: Find out the meaning of: disregard; preoccupation; theory; flimsy; rudder; ⁕gend; revolution.

⁕uestions: Answer the questions in sentence form where possible.

What feat is Daedalus said to have achieved?
How was Icarus killed?
What did the experimenters of the 18th century eventually come to realise.
Explain how the hot air balloon works?
Can you think of three reasons why hot air balloons are dangerous?
Who were the first aerial passengers?
What event occurred at Kitty Hawk on December 17th 1903?
Pretend you are a newspaper reporter who witnessed the first airplane flight. Write a report on what happened.

Asking Questions

Always begin a question with a capital letter and end it with a question mark.

(A) Write questions to which the following sentences are the answers. Use the words When? Where? How? Why? Who? What?

1. Because she missed the bus to school
2. The baby is two years old.
3. I saw the otter in the river.
4. It is a red car.
5. The birds sang at sunrise.
6. We picked apples in the orchard.
7. He escaped through a hole in the wall.
8. Because she has the measles.
9. John Bowman won the race.
10. The plane leaves at four o'clock.

(B) Write a question which you would like to ask each of the following people.

1. Christopher Columbus, discoverer of America.
2. A lighthouse keeper.
3. Neil Armstrong, the first person on the moon.
4. Marco Polo, the great explorer and traveller.
5. A policeman.
6. An Olympic champion.
7. The man who first climbed Everest.
8. The President of the USA.
9. The pilot of a jet aircraft.
10. Florence Nightingale.

(C) Write out these riddles correctly. Try to give the answer for each one.

1. What gets wetter the more it dries.
2. What gets bigger the more you take from it.
3. Which is heavier: a kilogram of stones or a kilogram of feathers.
4. What is made dirty by washing.
5. Which creature walks on four legs in the morning, two legs in the afternoon, and three legs in the evening.
6. Why did the chicken cross the road.
7. What is black and white and red all over.

Synonyms

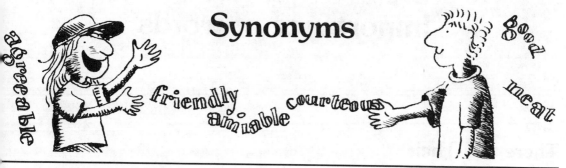

A synonym is a word that has the same or nearly the same meaning as another word. It helps you to avoid repetition of the same word.

agreeable	amiable	courteous
delightful	friendly	good
kind	polite	refined
dainty	fine	neat
tidy	trim	luscious
delicious	delicate	soft

(A) Choose a suitable synonym from the above list to replace the over-used word "nice".

1. My father prepared a *nice* meal of steak and onions.
2. The duchess wore a *nice* dress which had *nice* floral patterns.
3. The vines were drooping to the ground with *nice*, ripe grapes.
4. They were *nice* people and they welcomed everyone to the wedding.
5. The *nice* schoolgirl helped the old lady across the road.
6. It was a *nice* evening so the actor went for a walk with the *nice* young lady.
7. The beauty queen had a *nice* soft complexion.
8. The barber gave the young man a *nice* haircut.

B) From the given clues choose a suitable synonym as an alternative to the word "look".
List, glance, glimpse, gaze, peep, spy, stare, scrutinise, gape, leer, observe).

1. .... : to look briefly.
2. .... : to look faintly or partly.
3. .... : to look slyly through a narrow opening.
4. .... : to look sideways with a crafty expression.
5. .... : to look stupidly with the mouth wide open.
6. .... : to look closely and examine in detail.
7. .... : to look fixedly and with wonder.
8. .... : to look searchingly and intently.
9. .... : to look carefully and to observe secretly.
10. .... : to look fixedly and with the eyes wide open.

Just as there are many different ways of laughing, so too, there are many different synonyms for the word *"laugh"*.
List: giggle, chortle, cackle, chuckle, smile, grin, sneer, titter, snicker, guffaw, snigger.

C) Write each of the above words in interesting sentences to show that you understand the difference in meaning of the synonyms.

Importance of words

There and Their

(i) "There" is used with the verbs: is, are, was, were, has, have.
Examples: There **is** a pen on the table.
There **was** a pen on the floor.

(ii) "There" sometimes means "in" or "to that place".
Examples: I went **there** last week.
He did not know who was **there**.

(iii) "Their" means "belonging to them" and is always followed by a noun.
Examples: I found **their** dog that was lost.
Their pet cat ran up the tree.

(A) Fill in the blank spaces with either "there" or "their".
1. The swallows were .... with .... friends the house martins.
2. Some birds obtain .... food by digging with .... bills.
3. To .... amazement the penguins fluttered .... wings and waddled toward
   .... camp.
4. The killer whales seized .... victims in .... jaws and disappeared.
5. .... is a kingfisher on that rock over ....
6. .... were hundreds of crows flying home to .... nests in the wood.
7. The barn swallows built .... nests .... last year.
8. Scientists came to .... village to study .... habits and customs.

(i) "Among" is used when sharing something among more than two people.
Example: The teacher divided the sweets **among** the pupils.

(ii) "Between" is used when sharing something between two persons or things.
Example: The teacher divided the sweets **between** Tom and Pat.

(B) Choose the correct preposition "between" or "among" to complete the following sentences.
1. The miser found a gold ring .... his coins.
2. Harry left a little space .... each word and the next.
3. The twins seldom agree .... themselves.
4. The Irish Sea flows .... England and Ireland.
5. The two pirates divided the treasure .... them.
6. The captain divided the sweets .... the players.
7. The young dancing couple shared the prize .... them.
8. The coin was wedged .... the two stones.

Creative Writing

Write a short essay on each of the following titles.

1. Voyage into space.

Suggestions: .... astronaut .... space mission to ....
tearful farewell .... launch site .... strapped firmly inside ......
...... countdown .... terrific surge of power .... lift off ......
...... capsule window.

2. An encounter with a bull.

Suggestions: .... blackberry picking .... large field .... herd
of grazing cattle .... rows of juicy blackberries .... sudden shriek of horror
.... a huge threatening bull .... bellowed angrily .... eyes
flashing with fury .... charged wildly .... panic-stricken ....
ran for our lives.

3. The Accident.

Suggestions: .... overslept .... hurriedly dressed ....
snatched a quick breakfast .... desperate hurry .... dashing across the street ......
...... screeching of brakes .... car skidded .... struck a glancing blow ....
.... dazed .... ambulance siren .... stretcher ......
...... injuries not serious.

How do we know about Dinosaurs?

Comprehension

Perhaps you think that the exciting stories you have read about dinosaurs are fairytales. But, *accurate* information about them has been collected by people called **archaeologists**. These intelligent people are like detectives gathering clues and piecing them together as in a crossword puzzle. Sometimes they discover important clues while digging — bones, metal objects, and bits of pottery. These objects help them in their studies of the distant past.

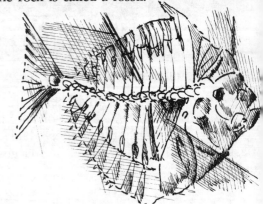

Many years ago in Northern Russia they found the remains of a huge creature like an elephant. It had thick shaggy hair and two curving tusks. It was a mammoth. When the animal had died it was covered over with snow and ice. This helped to preserve the mammoth in the same way as a deep freeze keeps the meat fresh. The animal had lain there for millions of years.

The study of fossils is another way to gather accurate information about the past. A *fossil* is the remains of some plant or animal that was covered over with mud and clay when it died. Millions of years passed before the clay hardened and was turned into stone. The *impression* of the plant or animal in the rock is called a fossil.

Perhaps when the fish in the picture died it dropped into the weeds at the bottom of a lake or sea. In time, more and more mud was laid down over the remains of the fish. Then only the skeleton of the fish remained, covered with *layers* of mud. After a long time the mud hardened into stone. The ground under the lake or sea was heaved upwards into dry land. The rock with the fish in it became high and dry. There is stayed until someone found it.

Dictionary work: Find out the meaning of the words in italics, and write each in a sentence of your own.

Questions: Answer the questions in sentence form where possible.
1. What work do "archaeologists" do?
2. Where were the remains of the mammoth found?
3. What helped to preserve this mammoth?
4. What is a fossil?

Activity: Each pupil in the class to bring in the oldest object to be found at home.
Example: watch, newspaper cutting, book ....

Each child then shows it to the class and talks about it.

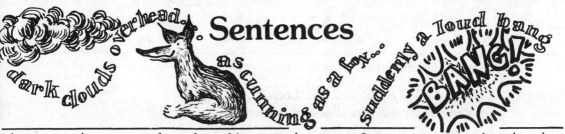

Sentences

A sentence is a group of words making complete sense. It expresses a complete thought. When you write a sentence remember:-

(a) It begins with a capital letter and ends with a full stop, a question mark or an exclamation mark.

(b) It must contain a verb.

(c) It must make complete sense.

(A) The following groups of words are phrases. They do not contain a verb. Complete each phrase by turning it into a sentence.

Example: just a second *(phrase)*   Just a second and I shall be ready. *(sentence)*

1. the crisp morning air
2. shortly afterwards
3. suddenly a bang
4. dark clouds overhead
5. as cunning as a fox
6. a wisp of smoke
7. in the moonlit valley
8. at the football field
9. the grinding of brakes
10. shrouded in mist

Short simple sentences can be extended and made more interesting by adding phrases. One helpful way of extending sentences is by answering the questions — When? Where? How? Why? What?

Example:	The horse galloped.
What horse?	The grey mare galloped.
How?	With a thunder of hooves the grey mare galloped.
Where?	With a thunder of hooves the grey mare galloped across the short cropped meadow.

(B) Extend the following sentences by answering the questions in italics.

1. Harry wriggled and crawled. *Why?*
2. The pirates hid the treasure. *Where?*
3. The little girl screamed. *Why?*
4. My father baked a delicious fruit cake. *Why?*
5. The diver found pearls. *Where?*
6. The detective arrested the lady. *Why?*
7. The dog howled. *How?*
8. Do not go swimming. *Why?*
9. The bird was singing. *How?*
10. A thick blanket of snow covered the countryside. *When?*
11. The wizard looked at her. *How?*
12. A blinding sandstorm blew across the desert. *When?*
13. I saw an exciting film. *Where?*
14. The truck swerved. *Why?*

Nouns

A noun is a naming word. It names some person, place, animal, state or thing.

Example: A **pack** of **dogs** frightened the **sheep** in the **field**.
Tom and **Mary** ate **pancakes** with their **friends**.
The **colour** of the **ink** is black.

(A) In the following passage pick out twenty seven nouns.

It was a glorious September day, with the warm sun shining brightly in the blue sky. High up in the air, the lark was filling the heavens with melody, and from tree and hedge came the sweet notes of thrush, blackbird and robin. The sheep were lying peacefully in the shade of the trees, and the cows were knee-deep in the river. Down in the valley, the machines were noisily cutting the golden corn; but louder than the noise of the machines were the shouts of the children, bathing in the cool pool by the ash grove.

(B) Write the nouns from the list into the correct blank spaces.

sovereigns	Larry	fort	girl
boy	cobblers	kingdom	hat
shoes	breeches	coat	toadstool
owl's	knees	purse	nights

Larry Leprechaun lives under an old ...... in the fairy ...... He is one of the fairy ...... and financiers. If you are lucky, you may spy him on moonlight ...... sitting on a baby ...... in the centre of the fairy fort. He is a pretty sight to behold, dressed in his green swallow-tail ......, little red pixie ...... with a decorated white ...... feather, ... buttoned at the ...... and buckled patent ...... Every ...... and ...... dreams of capturing ...... and his ...... of golden ......

Singular and Plural Nouns

A noun is in the singular when it names one person or thing. It is in the plural if it names more than one thing.

(C) Write in the plural of the following nouns.

Singular	Plural	Singular	Plural	Singular	Plural
branch	....	salmon	....	buffalo	....
face	....	child	....	ox	....
nose	....	tooth	....	deer	....
penny	....	cargo	....	chief	....
army	....	hero	....	hoof	....
cry	....	reef	....	piano	....
flea	....	echo	....	man	....
thief	....	dwarf	....	grotto	....
roof	....	fly	....	cod	....
potato	....	wolf	....	deer	....
woman	....	goose	....	volcano	....
mouse	....	foot	....		

The Bears
Comprehension

Suddenly, Ned felt that he must look over his shoulder. Whether it was that he noticed the bear looking at something beyond him, or that he heard sounds behind him, he was not sure; but he simply had to look round. If a man's hair can stand on end with horror, then, Ned Blake's hair stood on end. He was sick with fear; so shaken that he nearly fell off the ledge. For there at the far end, blocking his way, stood another huge grizzly bear.

Ned was so dazed with terror that at first he thought he was going mad and seeing grizzlies everywhere. Yet the two bears were real; and one thing soon became plain — he was trapped.

Desperately he looked down into the *ravine*. He would certainly fall and be *dashed* to pieces if he attempted that route. He looked up at the rock wall above him. It was so *sheer* that not even a monkey could have managed to scale it.

Bitter thoughts rose in the man's mind as he remembered his rifle lying in the *gorge* below. A *menacing* growl from each side answered him. Ned lost his self-control completely, and screamed and screamed again.

The next few seconds remained in Ned Blake's memory ever afterwards as a confused nightmare, ended mercifully by the touch of a *dangling* rope on his shoulder. Pulling himself together he grasped the rope firmly, and heaved himself up until he was half-way up the rock-wall and could pause, feet *braced* against the rock, and look down on the bears. Their growls became louder and angrier. Ned, not knowing that the animals were more interested in each other than in him, was faint with fear. When his brother finally dragged him to safety, he had only strength enough left to stagger away from the edge and gasp, "Let's go home."

The two bears advanced towards each other step by step — in no hurry, yet perfectly ready to fight.

Dictionary work: Find out the meaning of these words and write each one in a sentence of your own; ravine, dashed, sheer, gorge, menace, dangle, braced.

Questions

1. What was it that terrified Ned so much?
2. Pick out three phrases which show how frightened he was.
3. Two reasons why "he simply had to look round" are suggested in paragraph one. What are they?
4. "He thought he was going mad." Why?
5. "He was trapped." Explain in what way he was trapped.
6. "The animals were more interested in each other than in him." What does this mean?
7. Who lowered the rope to Ned?
8. Explain the following words, taken from the story.
   a menacing growl; a nightmare; a dangling rope; to scale the wall; the wall was so sheer
9. The hunter had a **strange** feeling he was being watched.
   Here are some expressions containing the word "**strange**".

strange land	strange face	strange to say	strange idea
strange house	strange character	strange story	strange writing

From the following lists choose an alternative word to replace the word "**strange**" in each of the above expressions.

surprising	eccentric	unusual	haunted
peculiar	novel	unfamiliar	foreign

Gender of Nouns

Gender of Nouns.

	Examples
A noun can be one of four genders.	
A noun that denotes a male is of **masculine** gender.	man, prince
A noun that denotes a female is of **feminine** gender.	woman, princess
A noun that denotes either sex is of **common** gender.	child, sheep
A noun that denotes neither sex is of **neuter** gender.	book, table

A) Write the masculine form of the words in italics. (Study page 95)

1. The *shepherdess* gave *Frances* a present of a *ewe*.
2. The *heroine* rescued the *landlady* from the *giantess*.
3. The *duck* and the *goose* attacked the *girl*.
4. The *manageress* ordered the *waitress* to serve the *lady*.
5. The *hostess* and *her daughter* welcomed the *duchess*.
6. The *lioness* killed the *hind*.
7. The *princess* spoke to the *mayoress*.
8. The *spinster* visited the *abbess*.
9. The *actress* and the *stewardess* spoke to the *empress*.
10. *Josephine's grandmother* was once a *governess*.

B) Pick out the nouns in the following sentences, and say whether they are masculine, feminine, common or neuter.

1. The policeman carried a gun in his holster.
2. The teacher watched the student enter the room.
3. The man shot the wild goose in the marsh.
4. The lady carried her handbag on her arm.
5. The birds built their nests in the tree.
6. The dog chased the cow into the field.
7. The mother left the baby in the pram.
8. The woman walked by the bank of the river.

Contractions

You'll see

You will see

I couldn't go

I could not go

It's six o'clock

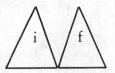

It is six of (the) clock

When speaking and writing we often shorten words by running or joining them together. These shortened forms are called contractions. Poets frequently use contractions to give rhythm and flow to their poetry.

An apostrophe (') is placed where a letter or letters have been omitted.

(A) Correct the following sentences, placing an apostrophe where the letter or letters have been omitted.

1. Dont forget to come early to the party.
2. Shes got the fastest motorbike Ive ever seen.
3. He doesnt know wholl be at the school drama tonight.
4. Theyll be late coming, so lets not wait.
5. Theres a ship I havent seen before in the harbour.
6. Id like to go to the play but Ive no money.
7. Were all going to the Halloween party.
8. If it isnt raining this evening, well go for a walk in the park.
9. We arent ready yet for the dance.
10. Whats the matter?

(B) Rewrite the following sentences, using the shortened form of the words in italics.

1. I *shall not* be able to go to the concert.
2. *It is* cold outside and *it is* raining heavily.
3. She *did not* know the correct address.
4. *He is* the tallest boy in the class.
5. *I am* sure *he will* come this evening.
6. *That is* the girl *who is* acting in the play.
7. *We are* going to visit our aunt's house.

Ain't

There is no such word, yet it is frequently heard in conversation. You should never use the word

List of common contractions

He's	he is	You're	you are	Can't	canno
He'd	he would	We've	we have	Aren't	are no
He'll	he will	What's	what is	Don't	do no

24

Creative writing

Write a short essay on each of the following titles.

1. A chariot race in Ancient Rome.

Suggestions: .... packed with people .... fanfare of trumpets ....
parade of chariots .... starting signal .... great roar of excitement ......
...... neck .... terrible collison .... one charioteer forges ahead ......
...... carried shoulder high.

2. Marooned on a desert island.

Suggestions: .... shipwrecked in a hurricane .... raft washed ashore ....
.. explored island .... built hut .... gathering coconuts and berries ......
..... made weapons .... hunting and fishing .... loneliness ......
.... lit beacon fires .... red sail on horizon.

3. A strange dream I had.

Suggestions: journey to a strange land .... tired and weary .... deep sleep ......
.... army of little people .... worked furiously .... tied down ......
.... struggling to break free .... flight of the 'little people' .... awoke from dream.

The Sun King
Comprehension

Stretching 4,000 kilometres along the coast of South America, the Incan empire of the sixteenth century was larger and better organised than any kingdom in Europe at the time. A road network of some 16,000 kilometres connected all parts, with messages being relayed to and fro by runners stationed every few kilometres along the way. For over one hundred years, a population of some seven million people was ruled by a single family of Incas, who had power of life and death over their *subjects*. Incas worshipped the sun and filled their temples with gold which they called the 'sweat of the sun'. The Inca, or king, was believed to be *descended* from the Sun god, and this explains the great power he held over his people.

A Spaniard, named Francisco Pizarro, had heard rumours about treasures of gold held by the Incas and was determined to find it and take it for himself. Hungry for gold, he set off for South America with a small force of 170 men. In 1533, after *enduring* great hardships, the Spaniards reached Peru, where the palace of the Incan King, Atahualpa, was located. The Incas were no match for Pizarro and his men, who easily cut them down with their guns. Atahualpa was captured and thrown into prison. What a *humiliation* this must have been for a king who once said: "In my kingdom no bird flies, no leaf quivers, if I do not will it."

Sensing the Spaniards' lust for gold, Atahualpa decided to bargain for his freedom. He began by offering to cover the floor of his prison cell with the precious metal. So large was this room that Pizarro was totally taken aback by the fabulous ransom offer and shook his head in *disbelief*. The desperate Inca misunderstood this *gesture* of Pizarro, taking it to mean refusal; so he now raised his hand above his head and said that, in return for his freedom, he would fill the entire room with gold to that height! A bargain was immediately struck.

Messengers were sent to the furthest corners of the empire with instructions for the collection and delivery of the gold. Within a month, the king's subjects had filled the room one quarter full with gold, worth £50 million. Atahualpa was true to his word, the Spaniards were not. Fearful of the *consequences* of releasing Atahualpa, the ruthless Pizarro ordered the execution of this last great Sun King of the Incas, on August 29th 1533.

Dictionary work: Find out the meaning of these words, and write each one in a sentence of your own: subjects, descended, endure, humiliation, disbelief, gesture, consequences.

Questions

1. How big was the Incan empire?
2. How did the Incas organise their communications in such a vast empire?
3. Why did Francisco Pizarro set out for South America?
4. How did the Inca or King, come to have such great power over his people?
5. Why do you think Pizarro's journey to Peru was such a difficult one?
6. How did Atahualpa try to bargain for his freedom?
7. Why did Pizarro order the execution of Atahualpa?
8. Pizarro was a *ruthless* man. Write six other words to describe the type of person he was.
9. The Incan empire stretched along the length of the Andes mountains in South America. Use an atlas to locate this mountain range.
10. Find out more about the Incas of South America, and write a paragraph about them.

Choose the Right Word

Said

Always try and give variety and colour to your writing by carefully choosing an appropriate verb. Many different shades of meaning are conveyed by using different verbs.

Rewrite the following sentences omitting the verb "said" and insert a more expressive verb from the given list below.

1. "Shoot!" said the captain of the football team.
2. "Where is the pop concert being staged?" Andrew said.
3. "In the Concert Hall," said Maria.
4. The manager said, "The show is about to commence."
5. "I did not break the window", said Harry.
6. "Good gracious!" said the lady, "I have lost my purse."
7. "My leg is wedged between the boulders," said the injured man.
8. "Don't make a sound," said Mr. Reilly, "the baby is asleep."
9. "I am going to win first prize," said Jim.
10. "If you rotate a coil of wire between two magnets," said the engineer, "it will generate an electric current."
11. "I work long hours and you pay me little money," said the worker.
12. "What a beautiful view!" said the tourist.
13. "Why did you not do your homework?" said the teacher.
14. "You are never on time for the rehearsal," said the producer.
15. "Doctor, come quickly," said the woman, "my daughter is very sick."

Alternative verbs for *said*

added	confessed	moaned	sighed
admitted	declared	murmured	snarled
advised	enquired	muttered	sneered
agreed	exclaimed	objected	snickered
announced	explained	ordered	snorted
answered	gasped	panted	stammered
asked	giggled	pleaded	stuttered
begged	grinned	promised	suggested
bellowed	growled	protested	surmised
boasted	grumbled	puffed	tittered
bragged	guffawed	remarked	urged
cackled	inquired	replied	warned
cautioned	instructed	reported	whispered
chortled	interrupted	retaliated	yelled
chuckled	interposed	retorted	
complained	informed	roared	
commanded	implored	shouted	

Kinds of Nouns

(i) **A proper noun** is the special name given to one particular person, place or thing that you wish to distinguish in a special way. These nouns are always written with a capital letter.
Example: John, London, Apollo V, Christmas Day, Friday, King Kong.

(ii) **A common noun** denotes no one person or thing, but is common to all persons or things of the same kind.
Example: man, country, boy, chair, pencil, woman.

(iii) **A collective noun** is the name of a group, collection of persons or things, considered as one complete whole.
Example: herd, crowd, swarm, pack.

(iv) **An abstract noun** is the name of a quality, feeling or idea. It relates to things which cannot be seen, touched, felt or tasted. It is not associated with any object or objects.
Example: poverty, health, height, revenge, flight, love, charity.

(A) Name the nouns in the following sentences. State whether they are proper, common, collective, or abstract nouns.

1. Pat and Kate went to the seaside.
2. Powys is a county in Wales.
3. She is a woman of great intelligence.
4. The chain was made of gold.
5. The dog likes to eat meat and chew bones.
6. Last Friday we ate fish for dinner.
7. Tom uses a tractor when ploughing but John uses a team of horses.
8. He managed to escape under cover of darkness.
9. Westport is a beautiful town in Mayo.
10. A plague of locusts ate all the wheat.
11. The boy chopped wood for the fire.
12. The Czar of Russia had great wealth.
13. Rabbits eat grass but otters eat fish.
14. We breathe air into our lungs.
15. The fisherman filled his basket with fish.
16. A pack of hungry dogs attacked the sheep.
17. The owner of the hotel is a wealthy person.
18. Joan kept her pet parrot in a cage.
19. The ship struck a reef but the crew was saved.
20. The ruler lives in peace and safety with his family.
21. It is a treasure of great beauty.

Startling Snakes
Comprehension

Snakes are fascinating reptiles. Their *flexible* scaly bodies allow them to live on land, in the trees and in the water. They are all able to swim but certain species do not like the water. The Indian python can remain *submerged* for over half an hour. Some of the big snakes eat enormous meals. They can go without food for as long as a year. The poisonous King Cobra of South East Asia, is capable of killing an elephant.

Snakes obtain their food in different ways. The boa family consists of the world famous Anaconda, the Python and the Boa Constrictor. These non-poisonous snakes coil their bodies around their victims and *suffocate* them to death.

Boa Constrictor

The boa constrictor is a native of South and Central America. It dines on birds, lizards and mammals. Having seized its prey with its backward-pointed teeth, the snake coils its strong muscular body around the victim. The terrific *pressure* applied causes the animal to suffocate and die of heart failure. Since the snake's teeth are unsuitable for crushing and chewing food, everything eaten must be swallowed whole. The amazing reptile can swell out its elastic jaws to surround and swallow a creature many times its own size. The skin between the scales stretches out to store the food. Powerful *digestive* juices in the snake's stomach help *dissolve* and break up the big meal. The snake usually swallows its victim head first. This prevents the fur or feathers of the unfortunate victim from sticking in the snake's throat.

Python

The regal python is the longest snake in the world. It grows to a length of 10 metres and lives in the tropical forests of South East Asia. Measure this distance in the school ground and you will then realise the great length of this reptile.

The female python lays between 4-100 eggs. After the eggs are laid she curls her body around the batch and rests her head on top of them. The mother python guards the eggs and the heat from her body helps them to hatch.

This huge reptile rarely attacks human beings. However, when threatened or trapped it is very dangerous. It kills its victims in the same way as the boa constrictor. It has been known to have killed and swallowed a 14 year old Indonesian boy.

A hungry python is capable of crushing and swallowing a young leopard or wild hog. Several days may pass before the enormous meal is digested. The juices in the snake's body help digest the animal, bones and all. After the meal the python becomes *sluggish* and sleepy. Then the intelligent hunter is able to surprise and kill this great snake. In some countries the meat of the python is regarded as very choice food. Its skin is highly prized and used to manufacture waterproof shoes, leather goods and coats.

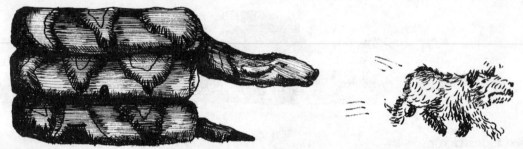

Anaconda

The anaconda is the champion of the boa family. This monstrous serpent grows to a length of 9 metres, slightly smaller than the giant python. The anaconda is one of the world's strongest and most heavily built snakes. One female *specimen* measured 1 metre in girth and weighed 55 kilograms.

The female usually hatches between 24-72 young snakes each year. Unlike the python, the eggs of the anaconda are hatched within the snake's body. She is one of the few snakes that give birth to living young. This reptile also holds the record for eating the largest meals. It can swallow a young deer. Dogs, pigs and sheep have also been devoured by this greedy snake.

Dictionary work: Find out the meaning of: flexible; submerge; suffocate; pressure; digest; dissolve; sluggish; specimen.

Questions

1. How do non-poisonous snakes kill their victims?
2. How does the boa constrictor seize its prey?
3. Why must the boa constrictor swallow its victim whole?
4. Describe the python.
5. If you were a hunter, how would you trap a python?
6. Why is the python considered valuable?
7. What record does the anaconda hold?
8. Which is the longest of the three snakes?
9. Give 3 reasons why you would/would not like a snake as a pet.
10. Write a list of (a) poisonous snakes (b) other reptiles.

The Apostrophe (')

The apostrophe is used to show possession or ownership. It avoids the over-use of the word "of" or the words "belonging to". We insert an apostrophe (') before or after the letter "S".

Rules

(i) We generally use an apostrophe before the letter S (**'s**) to show that something belongs to **one person**.

Examples: the girl's hat ...... means ...... the hat of the girl.

the boy's school ...... means ...... the school of the boy.

(ii) We generally use an apostrophe after the letter S (**s'**) to show that something belongs to **several people**.

Examples: the girls' hats ...... means ...... the hats of the girls

the boys' school ...... means ...... the school of the boys

iii) If the plural of the word does not end in S we add **'s** to denote possession.

Examples: the mice's cheese ...... means ...... the cheese of the mice

the men's hats ...... means ...... the hats of the men

iv) If the word already ends in S or a sound like S, we either: (a) place the apostrophe after the S or the S sound or else (b) we add **'s** to form an extra syllable in order to make it easy for us to pronounce the word. Usage of words is the best guideline to follow here.

Examples: (a) for goodness' sake, Moses' people, for conscience' sake, the Times' editor.

(b) James's Street, Jones's Road, Charles's death.

A) Insert the apostrophe in the following sentences.

1. The soldiers helmet lay on the table.
2. Marys friends arrived at the door.
3. Mr. Murphys cat and Mrs. Brownes dog were killed last week.
4. The ladies shoes and the referees coat were stolen.
5. Johns friend is staying at his uncles cottage in the country.
6. Mens hats and boys shoes are sold in that shop.
7. The pupils classroom is bigger than the teachers staffroom.
8. In his minds eye, the poet still saw the childs beautiful face.
9. The ships sail was torn by the strong wind.
10. Carmels sister formed a Girl Guides Club.
11. The cuckoo laid her eggs in different birds nests.
12. The babys nappies are hanging on the clothes line.
13. The suns rays shone on the waters surface.
14. The committees report praised the work done by the class.

(B) Rewrite the following sentences using an apostrophe to replace the words in italics.

Example: The *dog belonging to the boy* bit the girl on the leg.
　　　　　The *boy's dog* bit the girl on the leg.

1. The *prison for war criminals* was demolished in the explosion.
2. The *hooves of the horse* were cut and bruised by the sharp cobbled stones.
3. She bought an electric guitar in *the shop belonging to her cousin.*
4. The *recreation hall for teenagers* was badly damaged by fire.
5. At the jumble sale the ladies sold several *cardigans for men.*
6. The *names of the two players* were reported to the referee.
7. They sell beautiful toys and clothes in the *department for infants.*
8. It seems that the *sails of the boat* were smashed in the storm.
9. We enjoyed the *haunting melody of the orchestra.*

(i)　Its ...... means ...... belonging to something.
　　　Example: The bull tossed **its** head in the air and pawed the ground with **its** hooves.
(ii)　It's ...... means ...... it is or it has.
　　　Examples: **It's** a wonderful day.
　　　　　　　　　　It's been raining all night.

(C) Fill in the blank spaces in the following sentences with either "its" or "it's".

1. .... spines protect it from .... enemies.
2. .... not certain if .... leg is sprained.
3. .... a long way to Tipperary but .... worth going there.
4. .... time to leave but .... raining heavily.
5. .... a shame .... wing is broken.
6. .... summer and the swallow has returned to .... nest.
7. .... been a long time since we visited this art gallery.
8. .... white tail bobbed up and down as it scurried into .... burrow.
9. .... not often we have seen an otter in .... holt.
10. When .... winter in Ireland .... summer in Australia.
11. " .... been a wonderful evening," commented Orla, "and .... a pity we have to leave so soon."
12. .... obvious that the peacock is proud of .... feathers.

Note:
Who's ...... means .... who is or who has.
Example: *Who's* the young lady in the blue dress?

Creative Writing

A forest fire

Imagine you are a member of the fire brigade. Write a story about a forest fire you once had to tackle.

Helpful ideas and vocabulary

.... on duty at the station ..... 999 call ..... frantic citizen ..... forest fire reported ..... team mobilised ..... quickly boarded our engines ..... sirens blaring ..... bells ringing ..... through city streets ..... startled pedestrians and motorists .....

... outskirts of city ..... dense pall of smoke ..... pine forest ablaze ..... fanned by the breeze ..... spreading rapidly ..... houses under threat ..... terrified woodland animals ..... rabbits scurrying ... bounding deer .....

Officer in command ..... orders ..... rolled out the hoses ..... powerful surge of water ..... attacked the raging inferno ..... back-up units arrived ..... five exhuasting hours ..... faces blackened ..... inhaled smoke ..... fire under control ..... finally extinguished ..... fatigued ..... relieved .....

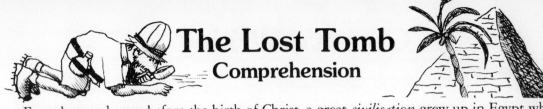

The Lost Tomb
Comprehension

Four thousand years before the birth of Christ, a great *civilisation* grew up in Egypt which lasted for thirty centuries. The ancient Egyptians invented paper and had already *developed* a detailed writing and measuring *system* at a time when others were still fumbling with clumsy clay tablets. They were the first to use locks and keys; they built the world's first lighthouse; they invented glass; and of course, they gave us the Pyramids, the first of the Seven Wonders of the World.

Throughout this long period, power was in the hands of a small group of Pharaohs, who were worshipped both as kings and gods. When a Pharaoh died, it was believed he simply passed down a long, lonely river to the underworld, to continue his life as ruler there. Therefore each Pharaoh had to be buried with all of his most valuable possessions, as well as enough food and drink for his journey to the next life. The buried treasure of Pharaohs was a great temptation to grave-robbers who, over the years, spoiled and *looted* tomb after tomb. Eventually, royal burials had to be undertaken with the utmost secrecy.

Many an archaeologist of the nineteenth and twentieth centuries spent countless and fruitless hours searching the valleys of Egypt for these hidden and long lost tombs of the Pharaohs. Howard Carter was one such person. He had spent seven years searching for the ancient tombs, and by 1922 was about to give up hope and pack his bags. Then, one morning quite by accident, he stumbled upon an opening in some rocks. To his amazement, he saw a stairway leading downwards! He entered with his friend, Lord Caernarvon, and soon they reached a room containing furniture which was proved to be 3,000 years old. Under the *flickering* light of their candles they were able to make out the entrance to another chamber. They made their way into this chamber where an *incredible* sight struck them speechless with wonder. The whole chamber glittered with gold — golden couches, statues of gold, and a magnificent golden throne. And, there in the centre lay a golden coffin. When they opened it their eyes fell upon the golden mask of a young Pharaoh, named Tutankhamun, who had died in 1357 B.C., after a short reign of only nine years. His was the only untouched tomb of a Pharaoh ever to have been discovered.

Dictionary work: Find out the meaning of these words and write each one in a sentence of your own: civilisation, develop, system, loot, flickering, incredible.

Questions.

1. For how long did the ancient Egyptian civilisation last?
2. In what way were the Egyptians more advanced than others at the time?
3. Name some other achievements of this civilisation.
4. Why was a Pharaoh buried with his possessions?
5. Why were the royal burials carried out with great secrecy?
6. How long did Howard Carter spend searching for these tombs?
7. What did he find in the first room of the tomb?
8. What did he find in the centre of the next chamber?
9. What was the name of the young Pharaoh who reigned for only nine years?
10. Imagine you are Howard Carter. Write a paragraph describing how you found the tomb and how you felt on finding it.

New Words

A) A journalist is a person who writes articles for newspapers. From the given clues name the occupations.

1. I repair steeples, towers and tall chimneys.   S ....
2. I am a legal person appointed to discover the cause of unusual deaths.   C ....
3. I sell flowers, wreaths and bouquets.   F ....
4. I am a person in charge of a museum.   C ....
5. I am the lady in charge of a hospital's nursing staff.   M ....
6. I load or unload ships.   S ....
7. I sell fruit and vegetables.   G ....
8. I am a male cook.   C ....
9. I look after people's eyes and prescribe glasses.   O ....
10. I preserve and stuff dead animals.   T ....

Note: Consult your dictionary for the correct spellings.

B) Write one word for each group of words in bold type.

Example: **The girl who played the drums** had long hair. **Drummer.**

1. He **made up his mind** to go to the concert.
2. The **woman in charge of the orchestra** bowed to the audience.
3. The music festival was **put off** until next week.
4. The pop singer **said he was sorry** for arriving late.
5. The singer was **worn out** at the end of the tour.
6. The **girl who played the piano** is my twin sister.
7. The **people in the church** listened attentively to the organ recital.
8. **All of a sudden,** there was a fanfare of trumpets.
9. He is **recovering his strength** at the hospital.
10. The composer wrote his **own life story.**
11. The festival of light opera is held **year after year.**
12. The flowers were **not real but made of plastic.**
13. During the performance smoking was **not allowed.**
14. Mozart's music is appreciated and played **throughout the world.**
15. Frogs and toads **go for a long sleep** in winter.

Girl who played the piano

Many English words are derived from the names of people and places.

sandwich: This word was "created" by the 4th Earl of Sandwich. During a lengthy gambling session, it is said he ate only slices of bread and meat to avoid leaving the gambling table. The "creation" of slices of bread with meat or other relish between them, gave the English language a new word — sandwich.

In recent years many new words have been introduced into the English language to express new ideas or inventions.

Example: Eurovision, cosmonaut.

C) Give ten other words introduced into the language in recent years.

Verbs

The dog chased the rabbit.

Most verbs are 'action' or 'doing' words. They are used to make a statement about a person, place or thing. A verb can be one word, two words or even three words.

Examples: The man **works** every day.

The man **is working**.

The woman **will come**.

Dublin **is** the capital of Ireland.

The house **has been sold**.

The lady **should have smiled**.

The dog **chased** the rabbit.

(A) Underline the most suitable verb in brackets.

1. The dark horse (ran, galloped, scurried) towards the final hurdle.
2. The mean thief (snatched, took, obtained) the old woman's purse.
3. The hungry hawks (swallowed, devoured, smothered) the dead sparrow.
4. The odd couple (strode, moved, strolled) along the beach.
5. The upset customer (argued, complained, grumbled) to the manager.
6. The timid rabbit (scampered, charged, flitted) across the meadow.
7. The brave soldiers (fought, defended, opposed) their fortress.
8. The cow (bit, ate, chewed) the cud.
9. The police car (bounded, screeched, glided) to a halt.
10. Clear crystal water (gushed, pumped, gulped) from the rock.
11. Forked lightning (struck, smashed, cracked) the clock tower in the village.
12. The injured athlete (gripped, groaned) with pain.

(B) Choose an appropriate verb to fill the blank spaces in the following sentences.

1. The car .... on the icy road.
2. The jet aircraft .... across the sky.
3. The nervous soldier .... through the jungle.
4. The audience greatly .... the concert.
5. The old steam engine .... along the track.
6. The agile dancer .... through the air.
7. The volcano .... during the night.
8. A thick blanket of snow .... the gardens.
9. The startled deer .... through the long grass.
10. The pilgrims silently .... their prayers.

36

An Intrepid Traveller

It was when she started reading books as a child that Dervla Murphy, Ireland's foremost travel-writer first developed an interest in and love for travel. Her father was the county librarian in Waterford and Dervla had access to a wide variety of books which fired her imagination for distant lands and her determination to see them for herself. Even as a child she would cycle widely in her native Waterford and as a young adult she made cycling trips to Europe whenever possible.

Dervla Murphy's first major cycling trip was to India. She made the journey alone, her only companion being 'Roz', her old reliable bicycle. After the journey she stayed in India and worked with the Tibetan *refugee* children in Dharmsala. It had been her dream to travel to India and now that this had been realised she set her sights on further horizons.

Three years later, she travelled to Ethiopia and made a long and dangerous trek across the Ethiopian highlands. At the outset, the rough terrain blistered her feet, forcing her to abandon her journey for a week. Her only companion on this adventure was a faithful mule called 'Jock'. 'Jock' bravely accompanied her for most of this *gruelling* trip, but due to *malnutrition*, he eventually had to be exchanged for a donkey. Although this was some years before the disastrous famine of 1985, food was very scarce in Ethiopia. Dervla herself lived on the Ethiopian diet of 'injara' and 'wat'. 'Injara' is a *fermented* bread made from 'teff', a cereal grain peculiar to the Ethiopian highlands. Dervla found it had a bitter taste and it took her a while to get used to it. Generally, the 'injara' is served with the 'wat' which is a highly *spiced* stew of meat or chicken.

Although she was robbed three times, she generally found the Ethiopians to be warm and hospitable. By the end of the journey, despite the fact that she could not speak their language, Dervla had developed a deep affection for these simple but noble people.

In 1979, Dervla set off to Peru with her nine year old daughter, Rachel. They spent four months crossing 2000 kilometres through the Andes, from Cajamarca in the north to the ancient Inca capital of Cuzco in the south. Once more, this was a difficult *arduous* journey which involved crossing swollen rivers, avoiding dangerous landslides, ascending steep mountain paths and descending into treacherous ravines. The breathtaking scenery of the Andes amply *compensated* them, however, for these discomforts.

Dervla was once asked why she undertook these journeys, which so often involved great physical hardship and discomfort. She replied that her idea of hardship and discomfort would be to spend a week in the Hilton Hotel.

Dictionary work: Find out the meaning of these words and write each one in a sentence of your own: gruelling, malnutrition, ferment, spiced, arduous, compensate, refugee.

Questions.

1. How did Dervla Murphy first develop an interest in travel?
2. How did she have access to so many books as a child?
3. What four continents has she visited?
4. What did she do in Dharmsala?
5. Why did her mule not complete the journey in Ethiopia?
6. What is the staple diet of Ethiopians?
7. Describe some of the hazards they encountered in the Andes.
8. Write a paragraph about the most interesting journey you have undertaken.

The Past Participle

(i) The past tense of a verb stands on its own.
   Examples: You came. She went. We sang.
(ii) The past participle requires another verb with it, some part of the verb "to be" or "to have".
   Examples: He has come. It was taken.

(A) Underline the correct form of the verb in the brackets.
1. They had *(come, came)* from miles around to attend the festival.
2. As soon as he had *(ate, eaten)* his meal he *(run, ran)* out the door.
3. We had *(swam, swum)* as far as the island in the river before he *(spoke, spoken)*.
4. The sheriff *(known, knew)* that the horse had been *(stole, stolen)*.
5. The boy had *(lay, lain)* there for hours.
6. If I had *(went, gone)* for the doctor in time the man would not have *(froze, frozen)* t death.
7. The old man *(knew, known)* that his daughter had *(win, won)* the prize.
8. When I had *(drawn, drew)* the sketch I *(gave, given)* it to the lady.
9. She *(written, wrote)* a letter to her friend but had *(forget, forgotten)* to post it.
10. The bicycle which he *(rode, ridden)* had been *(stole, stolen)*.
11. The boy *(ran, run)* away after he had *(broke, broken)* the window.
12. No sooner had he *(rose, risen)* than a fat rabbit *(ran, run)* across the field.
13. He had scarcely *(awoke, awakened)* when it *(began, begun)* to snow.
14. The coat he *(chose, chosen)* to buy was *(tore, torn)*.
15. The mayoress *(shaken, shook)* hands with the soprano who had *(sang, sung)* in th church.

(B) Complete this table.

Present Tense	Past Tense	Past Participle
They fly	They flew	They have flown
We know	....	....
You steal	....	....
She rises	....	....
He creeps	....	....
I wear	....	....
They forget	....	....
You draw	....	....
We awake	....	....
They ring	....	....
He speaks	....	....

The Rescue

Write an essay:

Helpful words and ideas:

sailing trip .... harbour .... life-jackets .... soft breeze .... sails fluttering gently .... skimming over the waves .... carried far out to sea .... without warning .... dark threatening clouds .... howling wind .... driving rain .... chopping sea .... boat lurching .... baled out water .... greatly alarmed .... signal flare .... crashing wave .... capsized .... swimming frantically .... stayed together .... clung to the boat .... situation desperate .... prayers answered .... lifeboat ploughing through waves .... hauled on board .... wrapped snugly in blankets .... anxious parents at quayside .... lesson learned.

Who First Discovered America?

Comprehension

On the 3rd August, 1482, three ships set sail from Spain with 120 men on board. For the first time, it was said, an *expedition* was sailing west across the unknown ocean, in an attempt to find a new passage to India. The ships were the Santa Maria, the Nina and the Pinta. Their leader was an adventurous Italian called Christopher Columbus. Columbus had found it very difficult to obtain a crew for his ships because people were convinced that the world was flat and believed that any ship sailing to the rim of the earth would simply *topple* over it into hell. In the end, he was forced to take convicts from the jails to man his ships. And after sailing for two months across this seemingly endless ocean, these men tried to *mutiny* and turn the ships back for Spain. Luckily, Columbus persuaded them to change their minds, because three days later, on the 12th October, they discovered land. Columbus believed he had reached India, and called the islands he found the West Indies and the people Indians. He had, in fact, landed on the vast continent of America.

But was he the first to discover America? The answer is almost certainly, no. Five hundred years earlier, a Viking sailing towards Greenland was caught up in a fierce storm and blown miles off course. He eventually returned home to Scandinavia with the tale of a new land he had spotted far away on the western horizon. The exciting news reached the ears of another bold Viking, Leif Ericson known as Leif and Lucky. It is now firmly believed that Ericson landed on the eastern coast of America, somewhere near New Jersey, around the year 1,000 and *established* a *colony* there named Vinland or "Wineland". This colony may have lasted for up to 300 years — nobody can be certain — until the *constant* attacks of *hostile* Indians finally forced the Vikings to set sail for home.

There are others who argue that America was discovered by the Irish saint, Brendan, five hundred years before Ericson. According to legend, Brendan had set out as a young man in a skin-covered boat, in search of a heavenly island on the western seas. His five year voyage was unsuccessful. When he was an old man, Brendan tried again, this time in a wooden boat. He set sail from Brandon Creek in Kerry, around the year 570, and during the two year voyage, is said to have landed on the shores of America.

The voyage of St. Brendan is surrounded by legend. The voyage of Ericson is cloaked in mystery. Christopher Columbus is honoured today as the discoverer of America. But the question will always be asked: was he the first to do so?

Dictionary work: Find out the meaning of: topple; mutiny; establish; colony; constant; hostile; expedition.

Questions

1. Why did Columbus find it so hard to hire a crew?
2. Explain how the West Indies got their name.
3. How many days did it take Columbus to reach America?
4. How did Leif Ericson come to hear of this new land?
5. Why do you think Ericson gave the name Vinland to his colony?
6. When and where did St. Brendan live?
7. In what ways did St. Brendan's second voyage differ from his first?
8. Who do you think first discovered America?
9. Trace out a map of Europe and America and mark in the routes taken by these three explorers as they crossed the Atlantic.

Quotation Marks

Quotation marks ("...") are used when writing the actual words spoken. We call this direct speech.

When writing the sentences only the words spoken are written inside the quotation marks.

Examples:

(i)   "I think those birds are swallows," remarked Peter.
      Peter remarked, "I think those birds are swallows".

(ii) "She is a great footballer," said Mary.
      Mary said. "She is a great footballer."

(iii) "When is the next bus due?" asked Tom.
      Tom asked, "When is the next bus due?"

A) Write out the following sentences correctly. Where necessary insert the quotation marks, capital letters, commas and question marks.

Who scored the first goal asked Michael.
Have you any old clothes enquired the old woman.
You have torn my copy book shouted Noel.
The taxi driver announced The cab is full.
Joan announced I like going to the cinema.
The man shouted Close the door after you.
Helen whispered The money is under the stone.

When you read the titles of plays, films, books, poems, ships and so forth, they are generally written in *italics*.

However when you are writing these titles, use quotation marks "......". The first word in the title and all important words are written in capital letters.

Examples: (i)   Louis Stevenson wrote the book "Treasure Island".
           (ii) Did you recite the poem "The Snare"?
           (iii) I have read "Huckleberry Finn", "Alice in Wonderland", and "Robinson Crusoe".

Study carefully the position of the commas and full stops in the above examples. Notice that all punctuation marks are placed outside the quotation marks.

B) Insert the quotation marks, capital letters and commas where necessary.

1. She christened the ship hibernia.
2. I went to see the pantomime snow white and the seven dwarfs.
3. Shakespeare wrote macbeth and hamlet.
4. At our local cinema I saw moby dick, jaws, and mary poppins.
5. Steven spielberg made the film raiders of the lost ark.
6. The twits was written by Roald Dahl.
7. Patrick Pearse wrote the poem the wayfarer.
8. Goldilocks and the ugly duckling are two well-known pantomimes.
9. Jules verne wrote twenty leagues under the sea.
10. John went to see the ballet swan lake.

More Quotation Marks

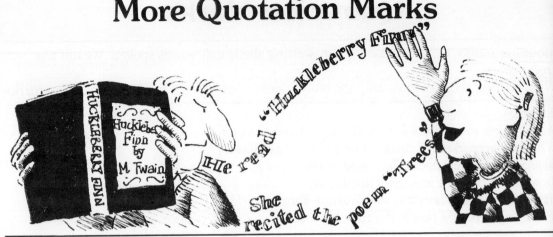

Remember: When writing the names of plays, books, newspapers, poems, boats, ships, aeroplanes, use quotation marks "...." and capital letters. Only the important words in the titles are written in capital letters.

Examples: I saw the pantomime "Puss in Boots".
He read "Huckleberry Finn".
She recited the poem "Trees".

(A) Insert the capital letters and quotation marks in the following sentences.

1. The princess christened the ship atlantis.
2. Daniel defoe wrote robinson crusoe.
3. He enjoyed the pantomime alice in wonderland.
4. She enjoyed reading the poem silver.
5. The dubliners sang molly malone.
6. We went to see the film moby dick.
7. The maiden voyage of the titanic ended in disaster.
8. I bought a copy of sonas magazine.
9. They named the rocket apollo, in honour of the greek god.
10. I like the cartoons in the irish times.

Quotation marks are also used when writing the actual words.

(B) Study page 41 again and then write out correctly the following sentences, inserting quotation marks, commas, question marks and capital letters.

1. Ciaran remarked the kestral is nesting in the ruins of kilrath abbey.
2. Tony inquired when will the new cinema open.
3. But that road is closed to traffic interrupted kevin.
4. Dress properly for the interview advised Roberta.
5. Why did dermot leave so early asked shane.
6. She recited the poem beautifully said cormac.
7. The singer complained the microphone was not working properly.
8. Maria requested May I borrow your spanish guitar.
9. We have the best hurling team boasted John.
10. You must answer the question ordered the judge.

Manu's Ark
Comprehension

Many peoples of the world have stories of a great flood. The oldest surviving work of fiction – 4000 years old 'Epic of Gilgamesh' - contains a story about a great flood and the building of an ark. This story is from the Hindu world.

The first man on earth, Manu, stood in a stream praying. Then one day a little fish nudged his ankle. 'Manu! Help! A big fish is trying to eat me!' Manu took pity on the little creature. He scooped it up in a pitcher. The fish began to grow. It grew and grew so he put it in a tank. It grew and grew, so he heaved it along to the sacred River Ganga. But soon it was squashed between the banks of the holy river. 'Take me to the sea', gasped the fish, 'or else I'll die!'

Manu prayed to Lord Brahma for strength, and then hauled it to the ocean. 'Thank you, Manu!' it cried. 'You have saved my life! Listen! Lord Brahma, the Creator, is not pleased with this evil world. He wants to destroy everything and start again. Do as I say, and you will be saved.'

Manu listened. Then he went out and built a massive boat. He went to every part of the world and collected the seed of every living thing, including the seed of seven holy rishis, the gods and the demons. He carried them all back to the ark, and waited.

Seven blazing suns appeared in the sky, burning fiercely. Wind and fire came like greedy tongues, licking round the world, gobbling everything in their path. Great, black clouds rolled across the sky. With a mighty crack, they split open, and down came the rain. The destruction began. It rained for 12 years and Lord Brahma destroyed everything except Manu and his ark.

Finally the rain stopped, Manu felt very lonely! The water stretched from one horizon to another. Suddenly, he saw a horned fish swimming towards him. Overjoyed, Manu swung a rope over its horns.

Year after year the fish dragged the ark across the never-ending water, until one day, rising out of the misty waves, Manu saw the tip of a mountain. The ark bumped to a standstill on the rocky slopes. Then the fish spoke. 'I am Brahma, Lord of all Living Things. I saved you from the flood, Manu, so that, when the waters drop, you can create life again.

So Manu set about creating all living things from the seeds on the ark. Soon all the rivers, seas, jungles and deserts were filled with life. Manu stood on the earth again and thanked God.

Dictionary Work: Find out the meaning of these words: pitcher, gobbling, overjoyed, demon, massive. Write each one in a sentence of your own.

Questions

1. Why was the little fish frightened?
2. Why did the little fish become a problem for Manu?
3. Who created the world according to his story?
4. What went into Manu's ark?
5. Who saved Manu from the flood?
6. Why was he saved?
7. Read again the story of Noah's ark.
8. List as many points of comparison as you can between the two stories. In what ways are they similar?

Adjectives 1

An adjective is a word which adds to the meaning of a noun or pronoun. It may go before or after the word it qualifies.

Example: **It is a warm** and **sultry** day.

The day is **warm** and **sultry**.

In your writing, choose striking and vivid adjectives. Descriptive writing should have all the colour and beauty of a picturesque painting. In the following passage study the choice of adjectives.

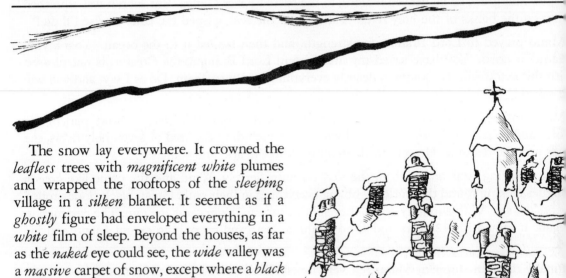

The snow lay everywhere. It crowned the *leafless* trees with *magnificent white* plumes and wrapped the rooftops of the *sleeping* village in a *silken* blanket. It seemed as if a *ghostly* figure had enveloped everything in a *white* film of sleep. Beyond the houses, as far as the *naked* eye could see, the *wide* valley was a *massive* carpet of snow, except where a *black* streak marked the course of the *drowsy* river flowing sluggishly westward.

If you wish to write exciting and imaginative stories you must avoid the monotonous repetition of the same adjectives. In describing a "giant python" you might write alternative words for "giant" and "python"! **Example:** monstrous serpent, slimy snake, loathsome reptile.

(A) Rewrite the following sentences using more descriptive and imaginative phrases to replace the words in italics.

1. The judge wore a *funny gown*.
2. It was a *fabulous show*.
3. She is a *lovely person*.
4. I like *sweet things*.
5. They are *nice people*.
6. Ruth had a *marvellous time*.
7. The dress had *pretty colours*.
8. It was a *very good game*.
9. The *bad* witch was *very cruel*.
10. The *brave* hunter tracked the *big animal*.

Advertisements are presented in appealing and colourful language to attract your attention. **Example:** fresh, dairy cream, frozen fish fingers, delicious juicy oranges.

(B) Draw an eye-catching advertisement with a descriptive caption in order to sell the following products:

Guitar, record, motor bike, perfume, shoes, rings, watches, shampoo.

Adjectives 2

(A) Write the following groups of words in interesting sentences.

Example: chestnut, galloped, colt,

  The chestnut colt galloped across the open plain.

1. timid, scurried, rabbit,
2. little, hopped, robin,
3. loathsome, glided, snake,
4. fat, trotted, pig,
5. tawny, flitted, owl,
6. angry, charged, bull,
7. clammy, leaped, frog,
8. faithful, barked, dog,
9. saucy, screeched, parrot,
10. ponderous, ambled, elephant,
11. graceful, glided, swan,
12. dainty, fluttered, butterfly,
13. gentle, soared, lark,
14. fallow, bounded, deer,
15. gentle, frisked, lamb,
16. hairy, swung, gorilla,
17. plump, strutted, turkey,
18. slimy, crawled, snail,
19. speckled, darted, trout,
20. grey, scampered, squirrel,

(B) Choose a suitable adjective from the given list to fill in the blank spaces.

Example: The **long, green** grass quivered in the **gentle** breeze.

black, yellow, brown, evergreen, grey, golden, hazel, red, white, speckled, tawny, purple, dark-skinned, fair-haired, pink, silver, green-eyed, sky blue, blue, piebald.

1. The gardener sprayed the ...... roses.
2. The ...... leaves withered and died.
3. The ...... trout leaped in the deep pool.
4. The elephant has ...... ivory tusks.
5. The ...... daffodils waved in the evening breeze.
6. The ...... beetle crawled under a mossy rock.
7. The bog was covered with clumps of ...... heather.
8. The ...... firs covered the mountainside.
9. The Vikings were ...... warriors.
10. The ...... owl hooted in the pine forest.
11. The squirrel cracked the ...... nuts.
12. The ...... natives swarmed around the boat.
13. A ...... mist hung over the valley.
14. The lark sang in the clear ...... sky.
15. The ...... stallion roamed the prairies.
16. The ...... monster rose out of the lake.
17. The hedge-sparrow's nest had four ...... eggs in it.
18. An Indian rode into the fort on a bright ...... pony.
19. The salmon's flesh is a ...... colour.
20. The ...... ears of corn waved gently in the breeze.

45

The Butterfly

Imagine you are a butterfly. Look carefully at the pictures. They will help you write the story. The first paragraph is written.

1. Born

I was born among the nettles. There I rested with my brothers and sisters, safe from the glare of the sun's rays and hungry blackbirds. At that time, I was about the size of a pin-head.

Gradually, I grew stronger and stronger and nibbled my way through the tiny egg-shell. At last I was a caterpillar!

2. Caterpillar

six legs ...... gripped firmly ...... crawled ...... munched juicy leaves ...... very hungry ...... powerful, strong jaws ...... fuzzy hair protected my body ...... grew bigger and bigger ...... swelled and swelled ...... burst and shed my skin (called moulting) ...... glossy new skin ...... grew fat again ...... swelled and shed my skin ...... this happened four times in all.

3. Chrysalis

(The pupa of a butterfly is called the "chrysalis". Pupa means "little doll".) One day I began to weave and spin a soft girdle of silk around myself ...... silk cocoon ...... cosy and warm ...... attached myself to a twig by a silky thread ...... I was now a chrysalis ...... rested and slept ......

4. Butterfly

awoke one sunny morning ...... magical change ...... a pretty butterfly ...... limp, feeble body ...... soft skin ...... stretched my wings ...... six slender legs ...... pair of feelers on my head (called antennae) ...... long curly tongue ...... flew about the garden ...... landed on a rosebud ...... sipped nectar from the flowers ...... drank silvery dewdrops ...... flitted and fluttered about the place ...... sunny days.

As Dead as a Dodo
Comprehension

In the world of nature, each plant and animal must try to the utmost to increase its numbers, in order to *enhance* its chances of survival. The elephant, the slowest-breeding of all animals, lives to about one hundred years and during this time will produce only six young. Yet, even at this rate, there would be 19 million elephants alive after 750 years — descended from only one pair. If this were allowed to occur, the world would very soon be overrun by elephants! The tremendous rate of increase in elephants, or any other animal or plant, is *checked* by a huge natural destruction of their numbers. Such destruction is carried out by the enemies of the particular animal or plant; but it is also caused by *competitors* struggling to get the same food or place.

If, for some reason, the destruction becomes very severe, the population of the *species* will begin to *dwindle*, and it may eventually become *extinct*. Extinction has been the sad fate of countless numbers of species. For over 100 million years, dinosaurs were masters of the earth, until suddenly, 65 million years ago, they vanished from the earth without trace. Scientists are still arguing as to how this extinction came about. Perhaps the flesh-eating dinosaurs killed off the vegetarian dinosaurs and then died of starvation themselves. Perhaps some smaller, more intelligent creature wiped out dinosaurs by eating their unhatched eggs. It has even been suggested that a deadly shower of meteorites from outer space may have been responsible for the extinction.

One case of extinction about which we have reliable facts, concerns the disappearance of a bird from the face of the earth only 350 years ago. For tens of thousands of years, the "Dodo" had lived a peaceful uninterrupted existence on Mauritius, an island in the Indian Ocean. It was a large awkward-looking bird — an appearance which earned it the name dodo, 'silly' or 'clumsy'. It couldn't fly either: it never needed to, because the island contained no *predators* that could threaten it. Then, in 1590, Portuguese settlers arrived. They brought many new animals to the island — dogs, cats, monkeys and pigs. These soon proved to be immensely harmful to the dodo. The monkeys started to steal its eggs and the pigs trampled on the nests, while the cats and dogs killed the young birds. By the year 1700, not one single dodo was left. The entire species had become extinct.

Dictionary work: Find out the meaning of these words and write each one in a sentence of your own: enhance, checked, competitors, species, dwindle, extinct, predators.

Questions

1. Why do plants and animals try to increase their numbers?
2. How is the rate of increase of animals controlled?
3. How does the extinction of a particular species come about?
4. When did the dinosaur become extinct?
5. What reasons are given for the extinction of dinosaurs?
6. Where did the dodo live?
7. How did the dodo get its name?
8. How did the dodo become extinct?
9. Write a list of species threatened with extinction in the world of today.
10. Locate the island of Mauritius in your atlas.

Adjectives 3

Adjectives formed from proper nouns begin with capital letters.

Example: The Spanish bullfighter married the Mexican dancer. *(Spain, Mexico).*

(A) Insert the proper adjective formed from the noun in brackets.

1. The shopkeeper bought a chest of ... tea. *(India)*
2. My aunt has a ... cat and a ... sheepdog. *(Siam, Scotland)*
3. I enjoy ... movies and ... operas. *(America, Italy)*
4. The ... restaurant serves ... cheese and ... wines. *(China, Denmark, France)*
5. The ... Government expelled the ... diplomat. *(Russia, Britain)*
6. We flew over the ... Mountains and the ... Sea. *(Wales, Ireland)*
7. The lady bought an expensive ... perfume. *(Paris)*
8. Switzerland is famous for its ... rescue climbers. *(Alps)*

(B) From the given clues introduce an adjective ending in - ous.

1. A sound with a pleasant *melody*.   A melodious sound.
2. A region with many *mountains*.   A ....region.
3. An artist who has achieved *fame*.   A ....artist.
4. A journey full of *dangers*.   A ....journey.
5. A child that is given to *mischief*.   A ....child.
6. An air crash which was a *mystery*.   A ....air crash.
7. A snake that *poisons* people.   A ....snake.
8. A tribe which *rebelled*.   A ....tribe.
9. A person always in good *humour*.   A ....person.
10. A blow given with *vigour*.   A ....blow.

Write down the adjectives formed from the nouns in brackets.

Examples: The baby's **childish** talk amused the adults. *(child)*

The **wooden** horse was left standing in the square. *(wood)*

1. The ...... nobleman helped the poor. (influence)
2. The ...... occasion was marred by heavy rain. (joy)
3. The old beggar was a ...... sight to behold. (pity)
4. The ...... warrior brandished his sword. (danger)
5. We were outnumbered and the situation was ...... (hope)
6. The ...... man dived into the river and saved the girl. (courage)
7. She is a ...... lady. (charity)
8. The actress lived in a ...... apartment. (luxury)
9. The .....child went to bed. (obey)
10. The ...... team paraded around the town.(victory)

Adjectives formed from Nouns

Noun	Adjective	Noun	Adjective
adventure	adventurous	joy	joyous
advantage	advantageous	labour	laborious
affection	affectionate	luxury	luxurious
angel	angelic	melody	melodious
anger	angry	mercy	merciful
anxiety	anxious	music	musical
attraction	attractive	misery	miserable
beauty	beautiful	mischief	mischievous
breath	breathless	mountain	mountainous
child	childish	mourn	mournful
care	careful	mystery	mysterious
caution	cautious	nation	national
charity	charitable	nature	natural
coward	cowardly	neglect	neglectful
comfort	comfortable	noise	noisy
crime	criminal	ornament	ornamental
critic	critical	peace	peaceful
cruelty	cruel	picture	picturesque
danger	dangerous	poison	poisonous
deceit	deceitful	reason	reasonable
disaster	disastrous	sense	sensible
energy	energetic	skill	skilful
expense	expensive	silver	silvery
faith	faithful	suspicion	suspicious
fame	famous	sorrow	sorrowful
fashion	fashionable	sympathy	sympathetic
fault	faulty	storm	stormy
force	forceful	success	successful
fool	foolish	sun	sunny
friend	friendly	terror	terrible
forgetfulness	forgetful	thirst	thirsty
fire	fiery	thought	thoughtful
fury	furious	truth	truthful
girl	girlish	value	valuable
giant	gigantic	volcano	volcanic
gold	golden	victory	victorious
grace	gracious	vigour	vigorous
grief	grievous	water	watery
hero	heroic	wisdom	wise
humour	humorous	wool	woollen
harm	harmful	wretch	wretched
hate	hateful	youth	youthful
influence	influential	year	yearly

Lovers of Nature
Comprehension

In *uninhabited* parts of the world birds and animals seldom flee from man. In fact many look upon men as strange visitors, and if they find that they are not *persecuted*, take little notice. But in all civilised parts wild creatures look on man as their greatest enemy, for they have always been hunted and killed, many for food, others in the name of sport.

Twenty-eight years ago my wife and I took possession of a small *tract* of land, about one and half acres in *extent*, on which there was a large bungalow. This was situated in the heart of sporting district where foxes, otters and badgers were hunted or trapped.

Being lovers of nature, we decided to attempt to make our small plot a sanctuary or place of refuge for all wild creatures. It was well suited for this, for three-quarters of it consisted of an old pit from which in the past sand and clay had been removed for making bricks. The sloping banks were over-grown with weeds, brambles and thorn bushes, while large, *lichen-covered* rocks were *embedded* in the soil. A thick *untrimmed* hedge surrounded the whole place, with here and there oak, ash and elm trees. The only thing lacking was a pond, so we made one at the lowest part, with a small reed-fringed island near its centre.

We proved that birds and mammals soon discover where they are protected, for after a few years our garden became a sanctuary in which all wild creatures found they were welcome. Thirty seven different species of birds have nested here and successfully reared their young and what is really more convincing, twelve *species* of mammals have brought up families, while five others have paid us passing visits.

In the springtime and early summer our *sanctuary* is filled with song.

Dictionary work: Find out the meaning of these words and write each one in a sentence of your own; uninhabited, persecute, tract, extent, lichen, embedded, trim, sanctuary, species.

Questions

1. Why do animals in civilised parts of the world flee from man?
2. What motives led the writer and his wife to take pity on the wild creatures of the countryside?
3. Which pastime, much practised by many other people in the district, was disliked by the new owners?
4. Name the features of the plot which made it well suited for use as an animal sanctuary.
5. In what way did the new owners make it still more attractive to certain animals?
6. What proof is there that the birds and mammals soon discovered where they were welcome?
7. Name six species of birds which might be seen in the plot.
8. Find in the passage words similar in meaning to: run away, shelter, taken away, buried, missing, find out, guarded, kinds, altered.

Expanding Paragraphs

By carefully expanding sentences we can make paragraphs interesting and exciting to read.

Example:

The robin tried to escape. She flew against the window pane. She fluttered against the curtains. She crawled under the sideboard. She lay there.

1. The robin tried to escape.
   The *frightened* robin tried to escape.
   In vain the frightened robin tried to escape.
2. She flew against the window pane.
   She *dashed herself* against the window pane.
   Many times she dashed herself against the window pane, *only to fall helplessly on the floor each time.*
3. She fluttered against the curtains.
   Rising from her last fall, she fluttered against the *window* curtains.
   Rising *weakly* from her last fall, she fluttered *blindly* against the window curtains.
4. She crawled under the sideboard.
   Panting painfully, she crawled under the sideboard.
   Panting painfully, she *finally managed* to crawl under the sideboard.
5. She lay there.
   There she lay.
   There she lay, *more dead than alive.*

The paragraph now reads.

In vain, the frightened robin tried to escape. Many times she dashed herself against the window pane, only to fall helplessly on the floor each time. Rising weakly from her last fall, she fluttered blindly against the window curtains. Panting painfully, she finally managed to crawl under the sideboard. There she lay, more dead than alive.

A) Expand the following sentences into an interesting paragraph.

1. It was a great circus. Every act was wonderful. I never enjoyed any entertainment so much.
2. There was no room to breathe in the shop. Customers crowded around. I was afraid I would faint. I tried to reach the door.

B) Build up interesting paragraphs from the following key sentences.

1. There were feathers everywhere.   3. It was a thrilling game.
2. He was a pitiable sight.   4. The thief was captured.

51

A Raindrop's Story

Imagine you are a raindrop. Write your life story. The first paragraph is written.

(i) "Pitter-patter, pitter-patter". Perhaps you felt a gentle drop of rain on your face as you hurried to school this morning. I always enjoy trickling down your nose and tickling you on the chin.

(ii) My home in the Atlantic Ocean ...... lived there ...... my brothers and sisters ...... tossing and tumbling ...... rolling and rollicking in the foamy waters ...... listening to the screaming seagulls ...... admiring the ships ...... watching the fishes ......

(iii) Warm summer day ...... strange magical change into water vapour ...... soared upward ...... explored the higher regions ...... journey across the sky in a cloud carriage ...... places of interest passed ...... sped over grasslands ...... bogs ...... saw and heard ...... glimpse of tiny houses ...... narrate an interesting or amusing incident.

(iv) Journey to earth as a tiny raindrop ...... in the distance ...... towering mountains ...... air grew colder ...... shivered ...... uncomfortable ...... millions of raindrops ...... space became congested ...... pointed my nose towards earth ...... dived ...... landed with a gentle splash ...... scurried away ...... swerved and dodged ghostly companions ...... the return journey to the sea ......

The Silent World
Comprehension

Instinctively I felt my comrade move close to me, and I saw his hand held out clutching his belt knife. Beyond the camera and the knife, the grey shark retreated some distance, turned, and glided at us head-on.

We did not believe in knifing sharks, but the final moment had come, when knife and camera were all we had. I had my hand on the camera button and it was running. Without my knowledge I was filming the oncoming beast. The flat snout grew larger and then there was only the head. I was flooded with anger. With all my strength I thrust the camera and banged his muzzle. I felt the wash of a heavy body flashing past and the shark was four metres away, circling us as slowly as before, unharmed and expressionless.

The blue sharks now climbed up and joined us. Dumas and I decided to take a chance on the surface. We swam up and thrust our masks out of the water. The *Elie Monnier* was one hundred metres away, under the wind. We waved madly and saw no reply from the ship. We believed that floating on the surface with one's head out of the water is the *classic* method of being eaten away. Hanging there, one's legs could be plucked like bananas. I looked down. The three sharks were rising towards us in a *concerted* attack.

We dived and faced them. The sharks resumed the circling *manoeuvre*. As long as we were a fathom or two down, they hesitated to approach. It would have been an excellent idea for us to navigate towards the ship. However, without landmarks or a wrist compass, we could not follow course.

Dumas and I took up a position in which each of us could watch the other's flippers, on the theory that sharks prefer to strike at feet. Dumas made quick spurts to the surface to wave his arms for a few seconds. We *evolved* a system of taking turns to make brief appeals for help on the surface, while the lower man pulled his knees up against his chest and watched the sharks. A blue one closed in on Dumas's feet while he was above water. I yelled. Dumas turned over and *resolutely* faced the shark. The beast broke off and went back to the circle. When we went up to look we were dizzy and *disorientated* from spinning around under water, and had to revolve our heads like a lighthouse beacon to find the *Elie Monnier*. We saw no sign that our shipmates had spied us.

We were nearing exhaustion, and cold was claiming the outer layers of our bodies. I reckoned we had been down over half an hour. Any moment we expected the *constriction* of air in our mouthpieces, a sign that the air supply was nearing exhaustion. When it came, we would reach behind our backs and turn on the emergency supply valve. There was five minutes' supply of air in the emergency ration. When that was gone, we could abandon our mouthpieces and make mask dives, holding our breath. That would quicken the pace, redouble the drain on our strength, and leave us facing tireless, indestructible creatures which never needed breath. The sharks' movements grew agitated. They ran around us, working all their strong *propulsive* fins, then turned down and disappeared. We could not believe it. Dumas and I stared at each other. A shadow fell across us. We looked up and saw the hull of the *Elie Monnier's* launch. Our mates had seen our signals and located our bubbles. The sharks ran when they saw the launch.

We flopped into the boat, weak and shaken. The crew was as *distraught* as we were. The ship had lost sight of our bubbles and drifted away. We could not believe what they told us; we had been in the water only twenty minutes.

Dictionary work: Find out the meaning of these words and write each one in a sentence of your own; instinctively, classic, manoeuvre, evolve, resolute, disorientated, constrict, propulsion, concerted, distraught.

Questions

1. Why, do you think, the two divers swam close together?
2. How did they defend themselves against the sharks?
3. Why did Dumas resolutely face the sharks?
4. What words in the story indicate that the divers were familiar with the habits of the sharks?
5. What do you learn about the character of Dumas and his friend from the above story?
6. What other danger, besides the sharks, did the divers fear?
7. Which sentence, do you think, is the climax or high point of the story?
8. Describe in your own words the emotions of the divers as the sharks circled them.
9. Give a verb similar in meaning to each of the following:- glided, thrust, dived, evolved, located, flopped.
10. Find expressions in the story to mean:
    (a) move back or withdraw
    (b) confused as to one's bearings
    (c) total loss of strength
    (d) cannot be destroyed
    (e) driving and pushing forward
    (f) agitated in mind
    (g) snatched or picked off
    (h) not expressing any emotion
    (i) with determination

Similes

A simile is a figure of speech comparing two unlike things and is generally introduced by "like" or "as".

Example: We had to turn our heads in all directions.
We had to turn our heads like a lighthouse beacon.

(A) Complete the following sentences by adding striking similes.

1. The rays of light from the camera penetrated the darkness like ....
2. The shark's fin cut through the water like ....
3. The diver emerged, gasping and snorting like ....
4. The sharks glided past like ....
5. The submarine rose like ....
6. The icy waters pierced my body like ....
7. The ship's shadow passed overhead like ....
8. Dumas resolutely faced his enemy as though ....
9. A dark shadow fell across us, it seemed as if ....
10. The men emerged from the water, tired and exhausted, as if ....

(B) Complete the following similes (if in doubt study page 94).

1. As sly as a ....
2. As sturdy as an ....
3. As silly as a ....
4. As white as ....
5. As hungry as a ....
6. As fast as a ....
7. As obstinate as a ....
8. As blind as a ....
9. As gentle as a ....
10. As good as ....

11. As cold as ....
12. As fresh as a ....
13. As timid as a ....
14. As black as ....
15. As fierce as a ....
16. As wise as an ....
17. As frisky as a ....
18. As tender as a ....
19. As stubborn as a ....
20. As sweet as ....

Meteorites
Comprehension

Our solar system is situated in the Milky Way, a galaxy with over 100,000 million stars. Our solar system, however, has only one star, the sun. There are also 9 planets, with 32 moons in all, and there are more than 100,000 asteroids. Some asteroids are over 100 kilometres wide; others are less than 1 kilometre wide; while others are only of rock or pebble size and are usually known as meteorites. They can fall at any time, in any place, in the world. Thankfully, they rarely do, although tonnes of stardust fall on earth each day without being noticed! Meteorites can be *composed* of iron, rock, or a mixture of both. For thousands of years, the iron was widely used by the Indian and Eskimo tribes of North America to make spears, knives, axe-heads and various other *implements*.

But when an asteroid or large meteorite does hit the earth, the results are *catastrophic*. Some 25,000 years ago, a huge meteorite crashed into the Arizona Desert, U.S.A., *gouging* out a crater 1,300 metres wide and 200 metres deep. It is estimated that 400 million metric tons of rock and sand were blown sky-high by the impact. *Fragments* of iron which were scattered all over the area were examined by scientists in the late nineteenth century and found to contain platinum, gold and microscopic diamonds. A mining engineer named Daniel Barringer was convinced that the priceless core of the meteorite was buried somewhere beneath the crater and was determined to find it. In 1922, he sank a number of drill-holes as well as half a million dollars — in a vain attempt to locate the meteorite.

The most famous fall of a meteorite in modern times occurred on the night of the 30th June, 1908. On that night, people all over Europe were amazed by the extraordinary *luminous* brightness which lasted throughout the night. From Russia came eye witness reports of a great explosion having taken place somewhere in Siberia at the same time. An expedition, led by scientist Leonid Kulik, finally found the place where the explosion had occurred. What they discovered was an entire forest — stretching for 30 kilometres — flattened by the blast. The damage was caused by a huge fireball from space, striking the earth at a *velocity* of 60 kilometres per second! Luckily, there has been no major fall of a meteorite since.

Dictionary work: Find out the meaning of these words and write each one in a sentence of your own; composed, implements, catastrophic, gouge, fragments, luminous, velocity.

Questions

1. What falls on earth each day without being noticed?
2. What is a meteorite?
3. Why were meteorites of value to Indians?
4. What great landmark is there in the Arizona Desert, U.S.A.?
5. When and how was this landmark created?
6. Why did Daniel Barringer begin mining operations in the area?
7. Why did Leonid Kulik mount an expedition to Siberia?
8. What did he find there?
9. Pretend that you witnessed a meteorite falling into the Irish Sea. Describe what you saw and heard.
10. Consult a book on astronomy to discover the difference between a meteorite and a comet.

Prefixes

He could not have picked a more unsuitable place. The opposite of the word suitable is formed by adding -un to the beginning of the word. The small word is called a prefix.

(A) Find a word with a prefix -un to complete these sentences. Use your dictionary.

1. The warning sign declared that it was un .... to swim near the rock.
2. He un .... the door and unleashed the Alsatian dog.
3. Mrs. Murphy's electricity was disconnected because her bill was un ....
4. The injured player was un .... to continue playing.
5. People who are un .... are not loyal.
6. The patient was un .... after falling from the ladder.
7. At the inquiry, many facts previously un .... were revealed.
8. Helen was un .... to fall and break her leg.
9. The ship's cargo was un .... taxes on the people.
10. The tyrant king imposed un .... taxes on the people.
11. We had to arise at an un .... hour.
12. The un .... spectators disrupted the game.

(B) Inter- is a prefix meaning "among" or "between".

Example: Waterford crystal enjoys an international reputation. From the given meanings find a word with the prefix "inter-".

Use your dictionary

1. a space of time between events.
2. to act between parties with a view to reconciling persons.
3. to mix two things together.
4. to meet and cross at a point.
5. to break in with remarks while another is speaking.
6. an exclamation mark or a part of speech.
7. a temporary halt or pause in a public performance.
8. to act as a mediator.

Write five words which contain each of the following prefixes.

com	in	trans ....
de	im	tele ....
dis	il	un ....
ex	pre	pro ....

Suffixes

A suffix is a group of letters added at the end of a word to form a new word.
Example: hopeless, assistant, hillock.

(A) Here is a list of the most commonly used suffixes. Try to make three words with each suffix.

-able	-ly	-er	-ous	-ess	-ion	-ible	-less	-ism	-ish
-acy	-ary	-ate	-ant	-dom	-ed	-ation	-ee	-fy	-wise
-en	-like	-ive	-fold	-form	-ful	-hood	-ician	-ment	-ways

(B) Find a word to match each suffix in the following sentences.

1. She earned a .... hood as a solicitor.
2. There will be many .... full candidates in the next election.
3. The .... less gambler lost a fortune in Las Vegas.
4. Our babysitter is a very .... able person.
5. The pupil was given extra homework because of his .... ish behaviour.
6. The .... ive model wore a beautiful evening dress.
7. The musician played a .... ly jig on the violin.
8. Stanley Baldwin was the leader of a great political .... ment.
9. The motorist was heavily fined for .... ous driving.
10. The brave .... ion of the fireman saved many lives.

(C) Choose the correct suffix to complete the words in these sentences.

1. The prisoner of war tunnelled his way to free ....
2. In order to start the machine you must push the lever in a clock .... direction.
3. Martin Luther was the founding father of protestant ....
4. The home .... man was given shelter for the night.
5. She was a very hard-working and efficient manager ....
6. He rang the office to in .... his employer that he was ill.
7. She sat down in a comfort .... armchair and read the newspaper.
8. The mission .... devoted his life to working for the poor.
9. They listened attentively as the story began to un ....
10. A cure for the ill .... has been late .... discovered.

The Voyage

Write an imaginative story about your departure on an Atlantic voyage.

Helpful vocabulary

1. .... gigantic liner .... as long as a .... as wide as a .... as high as a .... bustling quays .... loading and unloading .... passengers boarding .... chatted excitedly .... friends and relatives gathered .... whistles and hooters .... departure time .... hum of engines .... in motion .... waved farewell .... out to sea ....

2. .... explored .... long aisles and corridors .... plush carpets .... comfortable cabins .... many facilities .... busy crew .... introduced to captain ....

3. .... climbed up on top deck .... salty spray .... ploughing through choppy seas ...... school of dolphins .... land on distant horizon .... wide expanse of ocean .... glorious sunset.

The Great Escaper
Comprehension

Ehrich Weiss was born in Budapest, the capital city of Hungary, in 1874. Hungary was the home of the circus, and as a young boy he longed to join one of the many small circuses travelling the countryside. He *pestered* and *pleaded* with his parents until, in the end, they allowed him to leave home and join one. Ehrich began as a trapeze performer, but quickly developed an interest in magic, especially that form of circus magic known as "escapology", the art of escape. His hero was a famous magician named Houdan, so Ehrich now *adopted* the stage name, Harry Houdini, in his honour.

Houdini travelled to America where he began to dazzle and *dumbfound* audiences with his daring *feats* of escape. Neither chain lock or manacle could hold Harry Houdini. Many a convict would dearly have loved to possess his magical powers, for time after time he proved that even top security prisons were unable to hold him. In Washington Jail, he was manacled and locked, without his clothes, in "Murderer's Row". Within five minutes he had his cell door open and began unlocking all the other cells; a few minutes later, he arrived in the warden's office, fully dressed. In New York, they wrapped him in a strait jacket and hung him upside-down from the top of a skyscraper. Houdini escaped easily. But the Delaware River was not so easy: it was covered in thick ice when the handcuffed Houdini was dropped through a hole into its deep, freezing waters. Six terrible minutes passed before Houdini struggled to the surface.

His fame as a performer spread around the world. His escape stunts seemed so incredible that some people believed Houdini was a cheat, while others even accused him of using witchcraft! Houdini *steadfastly* refused, however, to *reveal* his magical methods. One of his regular acts was to show how he could take hard punches to the stomach without discomfort. Unfortunately one night, a student caught him unawares with a fierce punch, which left him badly injured and from which he never recovered. On October 31st, 1926, Harry Houdini, the great escaper, died.

Dictionary work: Find out the meaning of: pester; reveal; plead; feat; dumbfound; steadfastly; adopted.

Questions

1. What was Ehrich Weiss's first job in a circus?
2. Why did he adopt the name Houdini?
3. Why would convicts like to have the powers of Houdini?
4. What daring act did he perform from the top of a skyscraper?
5. What narrow escape did he once have?
6. How do you think Houdini could make such amazing escapes?
7. What unfortunate accident led to his death?
8. Name five other people who perform in a circus.
9. Describe what tricks you would like to do, if you were a circus performer.

Comparison of Adjectives 1

There are three degrees of comparison.

i) **Positive:** The simple form of the adjective to describe a person or object.
Example: Nora is tall.

ii) **Comparative:** The form of the adjective used when comparing two people or objects.
Example: Nora is taller than Mary.

iii) **Superlative:** The form of the adjective used when speaking of more than two people.
Example: Nora is the tallest of the three girls.

Rules for the formation of the comparative and superlative forms of adjectives.

i) Add -er and -est to the positive form.
Example: small, smaller, smallest,

ii) If the adjective ends in -e add -r and -st to the positive and comparative forms.
Example: brave, braver, bravest,

iii) If the adjective is a word of two or more syllables, we *generally* place "more" and "most" before the positive and comparative forms.
Example: beautiful, more beautiful, most beautiful,

iv) A certain number of adjectives are irregular and must be learned.

Example:

good	better	best
bad	worse	worst
little	less, lesser	least
many	more	most
much	more	most
old	older, elder	oldest, eldest
late	later	latest, last
up	upper	uppermost
far	further	furthest

Common errors to avoid

i) "Unique" has no comparative or superlative form.
Example: This book is unique.

ii) "Little, less and least" are used to denote quantity or amount.
Example: little milk, less sugar, less salt,

iii) "Few, fewer, fewest" are used to denote a number of people or things.
Example: few people, fewer corrections, fewer arrivals,

iv) "Elder, eldest" are used for persons of the same family.
Example: My elder sister is engaged.

v) "Older, oldest" can be used only for unrelated persons or things.
Example: This is the oldest car in the race.
She is the oldest inhabitant in the country.

Comparison of Adjectives 2

Choose the correct word in brackets to fill the blank spaces.

1. She is the ...... of the twins. *(biggest, bigger)*
2. Which is the ......, a giraffe or a camel? *(taller, tallest)*
3. The painting is as ...... as the photograph. *(beautiful, more beautiful)*
4. This boy made the ...... number of errors. *(fewest, least)*
5. Harry was ...... than his brother. *(more cautious, most cautious)*
6. The carpenter sawed off the ...... end of the log. *(rougher, roughest)*
7. There were ...... spectators than runners at the sports stadium. *(less, fewer)*
8. He is the ...... boy in the choir. *(smaller, smallest)*
9. The ...... team won the rugby final. *(best, better)*
10. Mary is the ...... of the two girls. *(younger, youngest)*
11. My ...... twin sister is in hospital. *(eldest, elder)*
12. The ...... away mountains are shrouded in mist. *(further, farthest)*
13. Which is the ...... subject to learn, English, Russian, or French? *(easier, easiest)*
14. My father is ...... than I. *(more wiser, wise)*
15. I have ...... records than you have. *(fewer, less)*
16. The teacher said our school was ...... *(most unique, unique)*
17. Niamh has the ...... end of the ladder. *(lightest, lighter)*
18. The four ...... players are being dropped from the team. *(best, better)*
19. Susan is the ...... member of the family. *(oldest, eldest)*
20. Here is the ...... antique in the museum. *(more ancient, most ancient)*
21. Harry held the ...... end of the rope. *(thickest, thicker)*
22. She takes a ...... lumps of sugar in her coffee. *(few, little)*
23. My penknife is ...... than yours. *(sharp, sharper)*

Adjectives		
Positive	Comparative	Superlative
small	smaller	smallest
red	redder	reddest
hot	hotter	hottest
bright	brighter	brightest
noble	nobler	noblest
crude	cruder	crudest
empty	emptier	emptiest
cosy	cosier	cosiest
dirty	dirtier	dirtiest
pretty	prettier	prettiest
lucky	luckier	luckiest
generous	more generous	most generou
cautious	more cautious	most cautiou
brilliant	more brilliant	most brillian
efficient	more efficient	most efficien
splendid	more splendid	most splendi

The Robin
Comprehension

The robin was now *exceptionally* tame, and never hesitated to come into the house and on to my knee or hand. He appeared on the doorstep about nine o'clock each morning, and would sing in the unmistakable *strident* tones of his kind for breakfast. One morning I heard an unusually loud burst of song from him. There he was, inside the front room, perched on top of a clock before a large mirror and singing his loudest at his own reflection, the feathers on the crest of his head raised in obvious anger. But he did not attack the reflection in the two or three minutes I watched him. Before many days, he had investigated every room on the ground floor.

The different notes he produced interested me. His loud *aggressive* song was very *familiar*, but often when he was feeding from my hand or knee, a number of cheeky sparrows would approach enviously, and immediately he would utter angry tic-tic-tic. Then again, if I made any sudden movement while he was on my knee, he would jump about a foot into the air, utter a sharp squeak and hover with rapidly beating wings like a tiny helicopter, before returning to my knee.

At the end of July, he was *moulting* and, in contrast to his usually *immaculate* appearance, was *bedraggled*. After another week, his appearance had become even worse. He had only one tail feather left. His breast feathers were still more bedraggled and of a dull shade of red. Four days later he was completely without a tail and no longer came up to the house. By the middle of August, however, he had a brand new tail and was as *spruce* as ever. His self-confidence and natural *aggressiveness* returned and he again chased away any sparrows that dared to come near.

Dictionary work: Find out the meaning of these words and write each one in a sentence of your own: exceptionally, strident, aggressive, moult, bedraggled, immaculate, spruce, familiar, aggressiveness.

Questions

1. How, in your opinion, did the robin know when to come for his breakfast?
2. In what ways did the robin show his exceptional tameness?
3. "One morning, I heard an unusally loud burst of song".
   What caused the robin to sing so loudly on that occasion?
4. Why should the sparrows be envious?
5. "He no longer came up to the house". Why not?
6. If you did not understand the word "moulting", you could make out its meaning from the paragraph. Explain how.
7. Write down words which have the same meaning as the following:- reflection, investigated, produced, cheeky, self-confidence.
8. Give one word having the opposite meaning of each of the following:- tame, different, loud, aggressive, approach.

Prepositions

The ball is under the table.

A preposition is a word placed before a noun or pronoun. It shows the relationship between the noun or pronoun, and some other word in the sentence.

Example: The ball is **under** the table.

The relationship between "ball" and "table" is shown by the word "**under**".

List of Common Prepositions

about	before	down	to
above	behind	during	till
across	below	except	towards
after	beneath	for	under
against	beside	from	until
along	between	in	up
among	beyond	into	upon
at	by	near	with

(A) Pick out the prepositions in the following sentences.

1. My friends and I are going hiking to Galway on Saturday.
2. The gold was in an iron box under the floor.
3. She received a letter from her friend in Paris.
4. The girl stood near the bank of the river.
5. John returned to work after a few days.
6. The call of the bugle awoke me from my sleep.
7. Fools rush in where angels fear to tread.
8. Millions of years ago, dinosaurs roamed about the earth.
9. The raft was swept downriver by the swift-flowing current.
10. The hare ran across the field and disappeared through an opening in the ditch.
11. Mary sat beside her friend during the concert.
12. Before descending, the helicopter hovered above the ship.
13. She left the office at three o'clock sharp and did not return.
14. I hid behind the tree and watched the soldiers marching across the bridge.
15. To whom were you speaking on the telephone?
16. Many domestic animals were drowned during the flood.
17. There is an ancient castle just beyond the river.
18. The foreign ship will not arrive till noon.

Note: Avoid ending sentences with a proposition.

The 300 Million Year War
Comprehension

Plants first appeared on earth 400 million years ago; insects arrived 100 million years later; d ever since, a fierce war has raged between them. At first sight it doesn't seem likely that the ants would stand any chance in the battle. Firstly, plants — unlike insects — can't move. condly, they are vastly outnumbered by the insects — an *average* oak tree will have tens of ousands of insects feeding on it. The great *naturalist*, Charles Darwin, once carried out an teresting experiment to show the extent of this destruction of plants by insects. He dug and ared a piece of ground about one metre square and then began counting all the tiny weeds as ey sprang out of the earth: out of 357 plants, no less than 295 were destroyed by insects. However, despite this fierce *onslaught,* plants are well able to fight their own corner and rvive. Scientists now know that plants have long been using deadly chemicals and poison gas *deter* their enemies! One type of potato releases a chemical that will kill any greenfly acking it. Tomatoes can release a gas to kill attacking worms. And trees produce a nasty ison, called tannin, when their leaves are chewed by hungry insects. Perhaps the most nazing defence of all is that used by the bracken plant. It will produce cyanide, the most deadly all poisons, when attacked by chewing insects. But it will allow ants to drink its nectar; while e ants, in return, fight off other insects that try to attack the plant.
A small group of plants have launched a full-scale *offensive* against their enemies in this :at war. These are the *carnivorous* plants that have turned to trapping, killing and devouring sects. In any Irish bog you will find at least ten types of carnivorous plants that need to feed on ects in order to survive in an area where food supplies are hard to come by.

ctionary work: Find out the meaning of these words and write each one in a separate itence of your own; average, naturalist, onslaught, deter, offensive, carnivorous.

estions

What is the '300 million year war'?
What advantages have insects in this 'war'?
Who was Charles Darwin?
What 'weapons' do plants use to defend themselves?
What did Darwin's experiment show?
When does the bracken plant produce cyanide?
Why are ants not poisoned by bracken?
What is a carnivorous plant?
List the names of any plants and insects you know.
Write an interesting fact you know about a particular insect or plant.

Prepositions 2

(A) Study the following prepositions carefully and compose a sentence for each.

1. accompanied *by*
2. according *to*
3. accuse *of*
4. agree *with* (somebody)
5. agree *to* (something)
6. aim *at*
7. angry *with*
8. ashamed *of*
9. blamed *for*
10. die *of*
11. die *of*
12. differ *from*
13. disappointed *with* (somebody)
14. disappointed *in* (something)
15. disgusted *with*

16. glimpse *of*
17. guilty *of*
18. good *for*
19. inspired *by*
20. involve *in*
21. invasion *of*
22. part *with* (something)
23. part *from* (somebody)
24. protest *against*
25. suffer *from*
26. satisfied *with*
27. taste *for* (food)
28. write *to* (somebody)
29. write *about* (something)
30. comment *on*

(B) Insert the appropriate preposition in the blank spaces. (about; to; in; of; on; for; with; by).

1. The woman was an authority .... flowers.
2. The teacher was proud .... his pupils.
3. The artist took pride .... his work.
4. The architect was opposed .... the building plan.
5. I have the highest regard .... my uncle.
6. He relied .... his wife for strength.
7. I was disgusted .... the man's behaviour.
8. According .... the doctor the patient was very ill.
9. The team was inspired .... its captain.
10. The journalist wrote .... the exciting motor race.

Creative Writing

retend that you are a parachutist. Write a story describing how you made your first arachute jump.

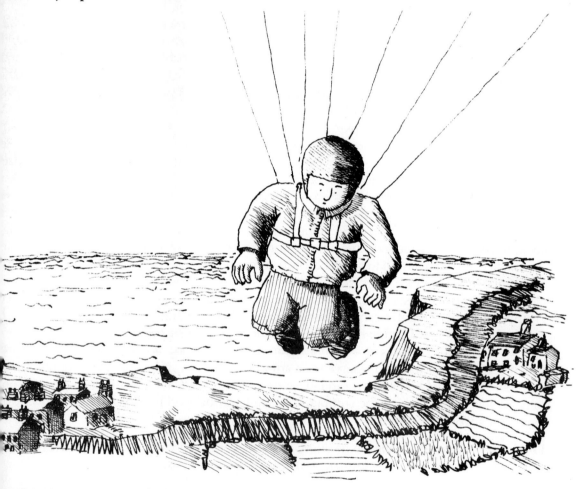

elpful ideas and vocabulary

.. arrival at the airfield ..... met instructor ..... advice ..... final rehearsal of parachute drill .. wrapped and packed the parachute ..... friends and well-wishers ..... twin-engined plane .. signal from the control tower ..... runway ..... engines roaring ..... thundered along ..... k off.

.. climbed ..... altitude ..... tense and nervous ..... pounding heart ..... hatch pulled open .. glanced down ..... hesitation ..... will-power ..... tumbled out ..... plunged ..... e-fall .... hurtled like a missile .... pulled the ripcord .... parachute released .... descending ely ..... floating gently ..... spectacular view ..... details of the landscape ..... drifting closer .. into a cornfield ..... hearty congratulations .....

The Computer Age
Comprehension

The needs of war have been responsible for many inventions, and the computer is [no] exception. The first computers were developed by the allies during the Second World War [in] order to crack enemy codes — a job they did very successfully. These machines were gigantic [in] size and extremely expensive. The computers of today are much smaller and cheaper, yet f[ar] more *efficient* and reliable. Over a short period of time there has been such a *drama[tic]* worldwide growth in the use of the computer, that now it can almost be regarded as an everyd[ay] machine. If you go shopping, it is computers which will probably have measured the amou[nt] you are given in each packet or tin bought; if you switch on a light, it is an ESB computer whi[ch] is regulating your electricity supply; or if you pick up your telephone, a computer can conn[ect] you to any part of the world within seconds.

There are two ways of looking at computers. Firstly, the computer — as its nam[e] suggests — can compute, or deal with numbers. This ability to do *precise* and comple[x] calculations allows scientists, for example, to work out flight paths for rocket probes into spac[e.] Without the computer, space exploration would be impossible. But the computer is much mo[re] than a brilliant calculating machine. Secondly and more importantly, it has enormous powers [of] storing and dealing with information. It is now possible for the information contained in eve[ry] book on every bookshelf in an entire library to be stored on a computer disc the size of a sing[le] book. In addition, any piece of this information can be got at within seconds and, if necessar[y] *transmitted* instantly around the globe. Such computers can be of great benefit to any larg[e] organisation. For instance, the police, at the press of a button, can have immediate *access* to ar[y] part of their files — lists of criminals, fingerprints, missing persons, owners of cars, et[c.] Furthermore, the computer can sort and compare this information, so that fingerprints can b[e] matched, or files *sifted* through to build up information on suspects.

With the aid of computers, a business can keep up-to-date *accounts*; hospitals can sto[re] patients' records; airlines can reserve seats anywhere in the world; banks can give out cash [at] any hour of the day; and schools can have a new and valuable aid to learning. These are on[ly] some of the ways in which the computer is changing the world of today. Who knows wh[at] tomorrow's world may bring!

Dictionary work: Find out the meaning of these words and write each one in a sentence [of] your own: efficient, dramatic, precise, transmit, access, sift, accounts.

Questions

1. Who developed the first computers?
2. For what purpose were these first computers created?
3. In what way are today's computers better than the earlier models?
4. Why do you think computers spread so rapidly?
5. Why are computers essential for space travel?
6. Explain how the computer is more than just a great calculating machine.
7. How are computers used in crime detection?
8. Give three other uses of computers in modern society.
9. Can you think of any disadvantages that might arise from computers and their use?
10. Describe the possible uses of computers in "tomorrow's world".

The Skelligs
Comprehension

A lone man, some 1,500 years ago, began it all when he climbed this rugged bird-haunted island and put down his *foundation* stone. He continues to amaze the architects, to defy the ocean and to *rejoice*, no doubt, in heaven at the triumph of his major purpose, which was to honour God in *defiance* of pirate and pagan. The Skellig, manned by three lighthouse-keepers, juts up among the breakers off the coast of Kerry. Here, a beam of light cuts a warning path in the ocean from the European window nearest to America.

On a day that scholars place as far back as the sixth century a forgotten monk climbed this *precipitous* rock and put a slate-like stone on a patch of grass near the two hundred and ten metres high summit. How he got there, up a hundred and eighty metres of jagged cliff on this dangerous rock, seven hundred and twenty metres long and three hundred and sixty metres wide, nobody knows. His foundation stone is there today, and so are the two spring wells that suited his purpose, the only wells on the rock.

The little group of houses he built with his colleagues on the Skellig, meaning a "reef" or "rock", about thirteen kilometres off the Atlantic coast, will *baffle* the curiosity of man until the end of time.

Merciless winds have ripped the roofs from modern stone houses at the base of the lighthouse, which stands on a seaward cliff. Atlantic gales and breakers have *marooned* the keepers for months at a time on this treacherous, bird-haunted reef. But the houses built by the early climbers, nearly 1,500 years ago, defy the Atlantic.

They are like domes, with a door at the base, built of stones that nothing is holding together, and that nothing except the deliberate act of man, can tear apart. Here they stand on the edge of a cliff in the *sparse* but *vivid* vegetation.

69

Dictionary work: Find out the meaning of these words and write each one in a sentence of your own; foundation, rejoice, defiance, precipitous, baffle, marooned, sparse, vivid.

Questions

1. Why do you think the "lone man" went to live on the Skellig?
2. How does he continue to amaze the architects?
3. What people now live on the Skellig?
4. What very important service is carried on there by these men?
5. What purpose did the two spring wells suit?
6. What tells us that the "lone man" was joined by others on the island?
7. How does the writer prove that the houses built by the early climbers were actually better constructed than those built in later days?
8. What is referred to as "the European window nearest America"?
9. What does the name "Skellig" mean?
10. Locate the Skelligs on a map of Ireland.

The tightrope walker walked cautiously

'Walked' or 'Went'

These words are too frequently used in writing. In the following sentences choose a suitable verb from the given list to replace the verbs "walked" or "went". Complete each sentence.

(marched, limped, climbed, strolled, plodded, prowled, stepped, crawled, raced, wandered).

1. The defeated team (walked) .... wearily ....
2. The soldiers (walked) .... quickly ....
3. The little baby (went) .... happily ....
4. The brave girl (went) .... courageously ....
5. The tightrope walker (walked) .... cautiously ....
6. The leading athletes (went) ....
7. The dark cat (walked) .... silently ....
8. The lost explorer (went) .... aimlessly ....
9. Napoleon (walked) .... triumphantly ....
10. The injured stallion (went) .... painfully ....

70

Adverbs

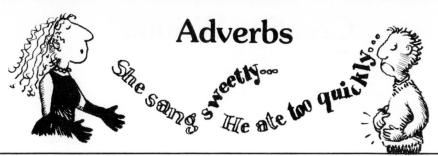

She sang sweetly... He ate too quickly...

An adverb is a word that modifies any part of speech except a noun or a pronoun. It generally modifies a verb and tells how, when or where the action took place.

Examples: She sang *sweetly*.   Modifies the verb "sang".
          He ate *too* quickly.   Modifies the adverb "quickly".
          She is *very* sad.   Modifies the adjective "sad".

A) Underline the adverbs in the following passage.

The house at the corner of the street was on fire. I hurried eagerly to the scene. The roof was ablaze. Men rushed frantically about the place with buckets of water. The fire was spreading rapidly, fanned by a still breeze. Blazing beams tumbled to earth as the flames greedily devoured the underlying supports. Showers of sparks burst brilliantly around in all directions, vividly illuminating the spreading shadows of night. In the distance the wailing of the fire brigade's siren could be clearly heard.

B) In the following sentences substitute an adverb ending in -ly for each phrase in italics.
1. The soldiers fought *with great courage*.
2. The doors were closed *in a hurry*.
3. The boy broke the window *by accident*.
4. The cat was lying *in peace* beside the fire.
5. The judge listened *with care* to the jury's verdict.
6. When the master of the hounds sounded the bugle-call, the dogs came *at once*.
7. Mary played the piano *with skill* and Joan danced *with grace*.
8. The gypsy looked *with contempt* at the handful of coins given to him by the rich lady.
9. Our aunt comes to visit us *now and again*.

C) Formation of Adverbs

Most adverbs are formed from adjectives by adding -ly to the adjective.
Examples: wise ... wisely; smart ... smartly.

Complete the following table

Adjective	Adverb	Adjective	Adverb	Adjective	Adverb
heavy	....	sweet	....	weary	....
faithful	....	happy	....	quick	....
certain	....	short	....	poor	....
humble	....	skilful	....	hopeful	....
obedient	....	simple	....	high	....

71

Creative Writing

Write an essay: A Lucky Find.

Helpful words and ideas:

Storm the previous night; went beachcombing; long sandy beach; screeching gulls; roar of the waves; lonely deserted sandunes; seaweed, driftwood, plastic containers; searched miles of shoreline; about to go home empty-handed; disappointed.

Just a few metres further; sheltered rocky cove; astonishment and delight; a yacht blown onto rocks; clambered on board; examined; mooring ropes snapped; signs of storm damage.

Hauled yacht to safety; dashed homewards; notified gardai; newspaper reporter photographs; grateful owner; big reward.

The Genius of Albert Einstein
Comprehension

People in ancient times were convinced that the centre of the Universe was the earth around which the sun, moon and stars revolved. When the great astronomer Copernicus proved that, in fact, the earth was merely one small planet revolving around the sun, it caused a great upheaval in human thought. Today, the people of the twentieth century can honour another man whose theories about the physical world are as brilliant and far-reaching as those of Copernicus. It is a curious fact that as a young German schoolboy, Albert Einstein showed such little promise. He was slow to speak and was considered to be dull by his teachers: he disliked memorising facts and hated the tough discipline of school. Yet from the beginning, Albert had a deep fascination and interest in the world about him. He once recalled how, at the age of five, he had been mystified and *intrigued* by the movements of the magnetic pin on a compass his father had given him. As he grew older, Albert Einstein decided to devote himself entirely to unravelling the unseen forces which move the world.

While working as an office clerk in Berne, Switzerland, he wrote and published a short paper entitled "The Special Theory of Relativity". This paper, written when Einstein was only twenty five years old, was to have a dramatic effect on man's total view of the physical world. His theory seemed so difficult and complex that, at first, few scientists could understand it. Indeed some scientists even *dismissed* it as the work of a fool. But experiments and discoveries soon proved Einstein to be correct. What he tried to show was that energy, *matter*, light, space and time are all related, and all *relative* to one another. In 1972, a unique experiment took place which helped to explain this idea. Four of the world's most accurate clocks, known as atomic clocks, were placed on board a U.S. Airforce jet and flown around the world. When the aircraft landed again, it was discovered that these clocks were running slightly slower than the clocks on the ground. In other words, time had slowed down on board the aircraft! This was proof of what

Einstein said sixty years earlier when he argued that a fast moving clock would run slower than a clock at rest. Put simply, time is relative to speed. He furthermore went on to say that, if a clock could move at the speed of light (186,000 miles per second) it would stop running altogether, time would stop. Imagine an astronaut setting out on a space voyage, who leaves a twin brother behind on earth. As the speed of the spaceship steadily increases, time runs slower for the astronaut than it does for his twin back on earth. And by this, time is meant not just the movement of a clock, it means the actual ageing of the spacecraft and the ageing of the astronaut's body. If the spacecraft could travel fast enough — say 99% of the speed of light — the astronaut could return to earth to find a twin who is now much older than himself.

It was his theory that unlocked the secret of the atom, showing the enormous amount of energy it contained. Tragically, this idea was used by other scientists to make the atom bomb, thus creating a great danger to mankind. Einstein was greatly saddened by this and time and time again urged world leaders to use peaceful means to solve their disputes.

He was awarded the Nobel prize and acclaimed around the world as a genius. But Einstein was a simple, modest man who *shunned* fame and publicity. He once said "It was only through ceaseless struggle that I was able, with my feeble powers, to understand these few ideas".

Dictionary work: Find out the meaning of these words and write each one in a sentence of your own: upheaval, intrigued, unravel, matter, relative, shun.

Questions

1. Why is Copernicus famous?
2. Many people were upset and confused by the findings of Copernicus. Can you explain why?
3. Why did Einstein not do well at school?
4. "Albert had a deep fascination and interest in the world around him." List some of the things that might have interested him as a child.
5. What did he write at the age of twenty five?
6. How did scientists become convinced that Einstein's theories were correct?
7. What does it mean to say that time is 'relative'?
8. What is the connection between Einstein and the atom bomb?
9. Find out more about the Nobel Prize and its founder Alfred Nobel.
10. Famous People:
    Write the names of any famous people you know under the following headings.

Scientists	Inventors	Explorers
. . . .	. . . .	. . . .
. . . .	. . . .	. . . .
. . . .	. . . .	. . . .

Artists	Composers	Athletes
. . . .	. . . .	. . . .
. . . .	. . . .	. . . .
. . . .	. . . .	. . . .

Confusing Prepositions

The abbess is in the garden

) "Past" is generally a preposition and is used with a verb.
   Example: The robber ran **past** my window.

i) "Passed" is a verb.
   Example: Henry **passed** his examination.

A) Choose the correct word "past" or "passed" to complete the following sentences.

1. The tawny owl swooped .... its nest.
2. My racing pigeon .... over the house.
3. The sick fox .... on the dreaded disease, rabies.
4. I .... beneath the low archway.
5. The bat flew .... in wide circles.
6. The circus was cheered as it .... through the town.
7. The ship sailed .... the lighthouse and .... through the canal.
8. The racing cars sped .... the grandstand and .... the finishing line ....
9. He is .... fifty and has recently .... his driving test.

) "In" shows a person or thing in one place.
   Example: The monk is **in** the cloister and the abbess is **in** the garden.

i) "Into" shows movement of a person or thing.
   Example: The rabbit ran **into** the burrow.

A) Choose the correct preposition, "in" or "into" to complete the following sentences.

1. She jumped .... the river and swam towards the boy .... the boat.
2. While the lady was: .... her office, thieves broke .... her house.
3. The rocket soared .... the air and went .... orbit around the world.
4. The otter swished its tail .... the rushes before plunging .... the river.
5. The boxer stepped .... the ring and became involved .... a dispute.
6. The sentence written .... French must be translated .... English.
7. Four .... twenty eight goes seven times, the number of days .... a week.
8. The magician changed the eggs .... the hat .... silver balls.
9. Looking .... her crystal ball, the old lady saw .... the future.
0. He held a stick .... his hand as he stepped .... the room.

The Pirate Queen
Comprehension

A woman in sixteenth century Ireland was expected to stay at home, rear children and be *utterly* obedient to her husband. One woman, who had different ideas and who became a legend in her lifetime, was Grace O'Malley. Certainly, Grace did marry the chieftain Donal O'Flaherty, she was a good mother to their three children, and she did her share of looking after and safeguarding their two castles in Connaught. But she was also a natural leader, who quickly became a power in her own right and who commanded the total respect and *loyalty*, not just of her own followers, but of many of the surrounding clans (or tribes) as well.

She was a skilled and fearless sailor, with an expert knowledge of the seas and rocky coastline of Connemara. With a force of 200 men and at least eight *galleys*, she soon controlled most of the waters from Mayo to Galway and Clare. Her living was earned by a mixture of *trade* and piracy. She sailed her galleys to Scotland, Spain and Portugal where she sold Irish goods and bought iron, glass, wines, silks and spices. Grace was also a *ruthless* and very successful pirate, who *swooped* down upon large merchant ships to either *relieve* them of their cargo or to demand a handsome fee in return for safe passage.

Grace was widowed around the year 1563. She later married the chief of the Burke clan and moved to Rockfleet Castle beside Clew Bay, County Mayo. At that time, the forces of Queen Elizabeth of England were struggling with great difficulty to remove power from the Gaelic chieftains and control Connaught. The activities of the pirate, Grace O'Malley, did not go unnoticed by them. In March, 1575, a large English force under a Captain Martin sailed into Clew Bay to capture Grace and her castle. With a great display of leadership and courage, she successfully defended her fortress for many days and finally put the enemy to flight.

Under Gaelic law, if a chieftain died, his wife could *retain* no more than one third of his wealth and property. In fact, it was often the case that widows were left with nothing. But when Grace's second husband died, she made sure that she kept everything by gathering her followers and marching away with 1,000 head of cattle! The cattle were not to remain in her possession for long, however, for the English were determined to teach her a lesson. Grace was eventually arrested and her herds taken from her. She now had to depend again on her ships as her only way of making a living. And earning a living on the wild seas became more and more difficult for an ageing woman whose every move was being closely watched. Grace decided to go to the Queen of England herself to argue her case. At the age of sixty three, she captained one of her own galleys and sailed around the south coast and across the sea to the court of Elizabeth in London. It was a dangerous and daring move, but it paid off. The Queen listened with sympathy and Grace's requests for the return of some of her property were granted.

Little is known of the remaining years of Grace O'Malley's life. Even her final resting place remains a mystery. But her name lives on in story and legend, and her fortress, Rockfleet Castle still stands proud and strong at the edge of the great ocean.

Dictionary work: Find out the meaning of galley; loyalty; utterly; trade; ruthless; retain; swooped; relieve of.

Questions

1. Where and when did Grace O'Malley live?
2. How did she rise to power?
3. How did she earn her living?

Why was her castle attacked in 1574.
Why did Grace march away with her cattle after her husband died?
Why did she travel to the court of Queen Elizabeth?
Why do you think the Queen listened to Grace with sympathy?
Pretend you are the captain of a merchant ship which was attacked and robbed by Grace and her men. Write a report describing what happened.
List the qualities that make a good leader.

B) "Whenever they made their appearance, a disaster invariably *took* place." The word "*took*" is used too often in conversation and writing. Choose an alternative verb from the given list to replace the over-used verb "took".

List

drove	stole	ate	won
accepted	drank	grabbed	caught
enjoyed	brought	picked	carried

1. He *took* the prize on behalf of his absent friend.
2. The thief *took* the lady's handbag from the counter.
3. The farmer *took* his cattle to the fair.
4. The worried mother *took* her baby to the doctor.
5. She *took* a hot cup of coffee before going out.
6. The native woman *took* the basket of eggs on her head.
7. She *took* the early train home from work.
8. The boy *took* the juicy pears from the top of tree.
9. The child's outstretched hands *took* the lifebelt.
10. The workers *took* a substantial meal in the evening.

C) The over-used word 'put'.

Avoid using this word in your essay-writing. Choose more exciting and interesting words.

Rewrite the following sentences, replacing the words in italics with one from the given list.
(written, postponed, save, reduced, surrendered, tolerate, filed, hoisted, elected, stored).

1. The price of bread will be *put down* from tomorrow.
2. The secretary *put away* the report in the cabinet.
3. The outlaws *put down* their guns.
4. She could not *put up* with the hustle and bustle of New York.
5. The pirates *put up* the "Jolly Roger".
6. The voters *put in* a new government.
7. Most of the novel was *put* very clearly.
8. *Put by* some money for a rainy day.
9. The warehouseman *put away* the goods.
10. The village fair has been *put off* for a week.

Pronouns 1

A pronoun is a word used instead of a noun.

Example: The woman spoke to Tom. The woman gave Tom a small parcel. Tom thanked the woman and hurried away.
The woman spoke to Tom. *She* gave *him* a small parcel. *He* thanked *her* and hurried away.

(A) Pick out the pronouns in the following passage.

"It is time for me to know you now. You are abusive and cantankerous like all pampered pets. Your forget the times I have saved you from the cat, who will some day kill you. Next time I see her stalking you I will leave you to your fate. And when any strange mongrels or pups visit the house I will not hang around like I do. Good day to you", remarked Fido to his friend Mrs Rabbit.

(B) Choose a suitable pronoun from the given list to fill the blank spaces in the following story.

List: we, myself, him, I, he, his, everybody.

...... said that Wopsy was an unusual dog. ...... thought so too. But then, ... was a strange animal. He had only one eye and one ear. However, all the children loved playing with ...... His colour was black and orange and maybe ...... was because his favourite food was orange peel. ...... were all sad when he choked after swallowing a goose's windpipe. My father buried ...... in a deep hole at the bottom of the garden.

(B) Underline the correct pronoun in brackets.

1. Joan and *(me, I)* went for a walk.
2. Who is there? It is *(us, we)*.
3. Give *(her, she)* the money.
4. The dog chased *(him, he)* and *(I, me)*.
5. He invited John and *(me, I)* into the shop.
6. The flood prevented *(them, they)* from proceeding.
7. It seems to be *(he, him)*.
8. Is that *(she, her)* in the blue hat?
9. He gave *(them, they)* to *(him, he)*.
10. He saw *(us, we)* in the street.
11. It now appears it was *(he, him)*.
12. She was certain it was *(they, them)*.

Creative writing

A) Complete the following story.

The old fortune-teller sat there in silence. She had enormous golden rings dangling from her ears. I was feeling nervous as I sat down. In a soft whisper she murmured, "............"

B) Complete the following story.

Foolishly I had taken my uncle's boat without his permission. I had scarcely reached the middle of the river when the fast ebbing tide gripped the boat. Too late I realised my danger.

C) Complete the following story.

Stealthily we tip-toed down the narrow winding staircase. The haunting silence of the castle sent cold shivers down my spine. Just as we were about to return Caroline cried out, "Look! a rusty door."

Two Great Buildings
Comprehension

The Empire State Building

The *demand* for space in the heart of New York was so great, and the supply of space so small, that the architects were forced to design taller and taller buildings. The *function* of the skyscraper in this the business capital of the world was simply to provide as much office space as possible. Although it is now no longer the tallest skyscraper in the world, the Empire State Building is still the best known of all modern buildings. It is 381 metres in height (448 metres if you include the television tower on top) and contains over 6,000 windows. Its 102 storeys have room for almost a thousand offices which receive 25,000 people on business each day. Each year its 62 passenger lifts carry *approximately* one and a half million visitors to the two large observatories on the 86th and 102nd floors. It is not unusual for these visitors to see it raining below them, while they are bathed in sunshine above the rain shower! Work on the building began in March 1930 and was completed in less than fifteen months — a remarkable achievement in such a short span of time. The cost of construction at that time was forty million dollars. The building *sways* slightly in strong winds causing its massive steel structure to *creak* softly. But building experts are confident that this skyscraper could cope with even the shock of a violent earthquake.

The Pyramid

The Great Pyramid at Cizeh in Egypt is an amazing sight to behold. Built four and a half thousand years ago, it stands as tall as a 40-storey skyscraper (160 metres), with a square base covering an area about 6 times the size of Croke Park. This building is so massive that St. Peter's Basilica in Rome, St. Paul's Cathedral in London, as well as three other of the world's largest churches could fit into it. It is composed of 2,300,000 blocks of stone, each of which weighs two and a half tons, and which were carved out of the quarries seven miles away. The blocks were then brought by barge along the River Nile and dragged by teams of men to the building site a mile from the river. It took 100,000 slaves almost thirty years to build this gigantic structure. Unlike the well-paid builders of today's skyscrapers who have cranes, diggers, electric drills and steel hammers at their disposal, the only tools these slaves had were levers and wooden mallets, copper axes and saws. The cost of construction is estimated to have been ten million dollars.

Probably the most startling fact of all is that the only *inhabitants* of the Great Pyramid were the dead! For pyramids were the tombs of the Pharaohs who for thirty centuries ruled a great civilisation which grew up along the banks of the Nile. A secret passageway leads deep inside to two small rooms in which the dead bodies of the Pharaoh and his queen were placed, along with their treasure and precious jewels. At least two million tourists flock to marvel at the Great Pyramid each year.

Dictionary work: Find out the meaning of: demand; function; approximately; sway; creak; disposal; inhabitants.

Fill in this chart to show the differences between these two great buildings.

	Empire State Building	Great Pyramid
Age		
Location		
Height		
Purpose for which it was built		
Length of construction		
Cost of construction		
Tools and equipment used		
Materials used		
Workers who built it		
Occupiers		
Number of visitors each year		
Any special fact		

Questions (give reasons for your answers)

1. Which is the largest building?
2. Which building will last the longest?
3. Which building do you admire most?

Pronouns 2

"I" and "Me"

Rules

(i)   After the verb *"to be"* use *"I"*. It is *I* who knocked.
(ii) After prepositions use *"me"*. The lion stared at *me*.
(iii) After *"let"* and *"between"* use *me*. The money was divided between Bill and *me*.

(A) Fill in the blank spaces in the following sentences with either "I" or "me".

1. She gave .... a sweet and .... gave her an orange.
2. Let you and .... go to the cinema tonight.
3. He pushed .... and .... stumbled.
4. Mary and .... played chess.
5. Mother divided the sweets between Jill and ....
6. Mary is older than .... but .... am stronger than she.
7. The ball hopped between Tim and .... but .... caught it.
8. The headmistress told .... to go home and .... went.
9. The angry cow chased .... and .... jumped over the ditch.
10. My brother is nearly as tall as ....
11. Rory is older than .... but .... am younger than Fiona.
12. Let Charles and .... work together.
13. She is almost as big as ....
14. The teacher asked .... to do the sum on the board and .... did it.
15. It is .... who called to see you last night.
16. Do you think it was .... who stole your pencil?
17. I am certain that it was not .... who did it.
18. That dress fits her better than ....
19. She gave .... an apple and .... bought her an ice cream.

The relative pronoun 'who'

(A) Use the relative pronoun 'who' to make ten sentences out of these statements.

1. The passenger left Dublin airport at six. He arrived in Heathrow an hour later.
2. The lady brought the cake. She is in the kitchen.
3. The garda rescued the old man. He was awarded a medal for bravery.
4. The boy stole the apples. He was caught by the gardener.
5. The politician appeared on television. She defended the government.
6. The child ran across the road. He was knocked down by a car.
7. The girl trained every day. She won the gold medal.
8. The surgeon did the operation. He spoke to the patient that evening.
9. The little boy lost his schoolbag. He was crying in the yard.
10. The centre forward scored the goal. He was congratulated by his captain.

A River I Know

Complete the following story. The first paragraph is written.

1. High up in the grey limestone mountain a tiny spring trickles out of a crystal-clear pool. With merry laughter the new-born stream leaps and tumbles over rocks and boulders on its journey to the sea.

2. flows through meadowlands ...... wooded valleys ...... sleepy villages ...... busy towns ...... cattle knee-deep in its cool waters ...... trout and salmon ...... young children swim and play in its waters ...... fishermen ...... sailing boats ...... modern bridges span the river ......

3. rushes through deep ravines ...... leaps in fury over a waterfall ...... joined by many tributaries ...... gathers strength and fury ...... plunges onwards ...... with a roar of joy flings itself into the ocean ......

Use the following opening phrases to begin sentences in your story.

Here it	After	On approaching the ....
Before it enters	Onward it flows	Continuing its journey ......
Rushing forward	Rushing onward	Eventually ....
Finally	At last	Breathless it ....

The Boy Who Saved A Swan

Comprehension

2500 years ago in India, there lived a very wise man. He spent his life teaching people how they should live and how they could end unhappiness. His name was Siddhartha Guatama, but most people called him the Budda which means 'The Enlightened One'. This is one of many stories about his early life.

Long ago in the land of India there lived a king and queen. They were very happy when their first son was born. They called the boy Siddhartha. The king was very pleased.

"Now I have a son to rule over my kingdom after I die,"he said.

Siddhartha grew up to be a strong boy. He had many friends. One of their favourite activities was to go hunting for deer. However, once when he and his friends had caught a deer, Siddhartha could see how frightened the animal was and he decided to let it go free. He was concerned that the deer might be hurt and feel pain because of their fun.

Once when Siddhartha was still a boy he felt pain himself for the very first time. He was playing in the royal gardens next to the palace with his cousin, Devadatta. A flock of wild swans flew overhead. They were migrating to the mountains to escape the high temperatures of the coming summer. The beautiful white birds called to each other as they flew across the clear blue sky.

Devadatta picked up his bow and took aim at the birds. The arrow hit one of the swans directly on one of its great white wings. The swan could not fly on any more and fell to the ground among the sweet-scented roses of the palace gardens. There it lay quiet and still with its white wing spotted with blood. The arrow was still embedded in the wing.

Siddhartha ran to the wounded bird. The swan was frightened and snapped its beak and flapped its uninjured wing at him. Siddhartha did not mind. He gently lifted the swan onto his lap and stroked it gently with his left hand while with his right he carefully pulled out the arrow. He poured honey onto the wound and covered it with makeshift bandages of leaves to keep it cool.

Siddhartha sat there comforting the wounded swan for some time. He wondered how the arrow had felt when it entered the wing. Siddhartha had never felt pain. He pressed the sharp point of the arrow into his own arm. The pain was great as the point cut the skin. There were tears in Siddhartha's eyes as he comforted the wounded swan.

After shooting the swan, Devadatta had gone home. Later that day he sent a messenger to Siddhartha.

"O Siddhartha, said the messenger, "Prince Devadatta would like the body of the swan for a feast. Please will you give it to him?"

"No," replied Siddhartha, "If the swan was dead then the body would belong to the person that killed it, but the bird is not dead. I have cared for it and am looking after it, the swan is mine. If my cousin does not agree with me then let him call the wise men together and let them decide who should have the swan."

Devadatta did not agree and so he called a meeting of the wise men. After much discussion their leader announced,

"Siddhartha has saved the swan's life by loving and caring for it. The swan is his by right. Devadatta has no right to the bird.

So Siddhartha kept the swan. He looked after it until its wing had healed sufficiently for it to fly away to the mountains.

Dictionary work: Find out the meaning of: announced, sufficiently, makeshift, embedded, migrating.
Write each word in a sentence of your own.

Questions
1. What were Siddhartha's favourite pastimes?
2. Why was the king pleased to have a son?
3. Why did Siddhartha free the deer?
4. Why did Siddhartha press the arrow into his own arm?
5. How did Siddhartha treat the injured swan?
6. Why did Devadatta want the swan?
7. Why was Devadatta not entitled to keep the swan?
8. What do you think Siddhartha learned from this incident?
9. How might this have changed his behaviour?
10. What do you think about the rights and wrongs of hunting animals?

Conjunctions

A conjunction is a word used to join words, phrases and sentences together. It can come either at the start of a sentence or between groups of words in the sentence.

Examples: Tom **and** Pat are friends.
Peter will begin painting **when** they leave.
Peter began painting, **so** they left.

and	but	either (or)	neither (nor)	while
after	both	for	since	when
although	because	if	unless	whereas
as	before	least	until	yet

(A) Choose one of the conjunctions from the above list to complete the following sentences.

1. The ship will not sail .... all the cargo has been unloaded.
2. Margaret passed her examination .... she never seemed to study.
3. The referee looked at his watch .... blowing his whistle.
4. The tenants hate the landlord .... he is a cruel master.
5. John will sing .... you play the piano.
6. Our cat has a long tail .... a Manx cat has none.
7. He thought the book was stolen .... he had given it to his friend.
8. My brother is going to buy either a guitar .... a record player.
9. .... there is no electricity he will have to use candles.
10. .... the wall is dry we shall begin painting.
11. The champion boxer was neither proud .... boastful.

86

The conjunction 'when' can be used to join two simple sentences.

Example: The boy ran across the road.

The motorist swerved to avoid him.

These sentences are now joined by **'when'** to give:

When the boy ran across the road, the motorist swerved to avoid him.

*Notice that a comma is placed in the new sentence between the two statements.)

A) Use the conjunction 'when' to join the following sentences. Remember to insert the comma.

1. Dick arrived at the station. The Train had gone.
2. The dog did not stop barking. His master became angry.
3. The snow began to fall. The farmer went looking for his sheep.
4. The lion escaped. Panic spread through the town.
5. The referee blew his whistle. The game was finally over.
6. The farmer appeared with his gun. The foxes fled in terror.
7. Patrick left school at eighteen. He joined the army.
8. The children heard the loud clap of thunder. They became frightened.
9. Gold was discovered in the valley. The news spread like wildfire.
0. The ice had finally melted. A golden daffodil appeared.

B) Complete the following sentences, all of which begin with conjunctions.

1. **As** soon as the bell rang ....
2. **Since** it is still raining ....
3. **After** the war was over, ...
4. **Until** I give the signal, ...
5. **If** you sell the bike for me, ...
6. **Because** they did not like him, ...
7. **When** the party was over, ...
8. **While** the engine was still running, ...
9. **Although** you do not believe me, ...
0. **Before** I travel to America, ...

C) Choose an appropriate conjunction and phrase to begin the following sentences.

1. .... , and we all went home happily.
2. .... , the children sneaked into the orchard.
3. .... , she cried bitterly.
4. .... , remain in your seats.
5. .... , I ran a lap of honour.
6. .... , the police arrived outside the bank.
7. .... , Pat said farewell to her friends.

87

A Cycling Trip

Write a descriptive story about a cycling trip with your friends.

A Vocabulary of Words

glorious afternoon .... gentle breeze .... fleecy white clouds .... destination .... peace and contentment .... hum and drone of insects .... wooded hillside .... stately pines .... grove of silver-grey birch .... purple heather in bloom .... rushing mountain stream .... sparkling blue lake .... ruins of an old castle .... shrouded peak tops .... pearly haze .... natural trail .... explored hidden paths .... enjoyable afternoon .... the return journey ....

Opening sentences that give variety to your essay-writing.

In the distance	Breathless we ....
On reaching the	Continuing ....
Here the	As we ....
Dismounting, ...	Occasionally ....
After a short rest	On approaching the ....
It seemed	Leaving the ....
After some time	Eventually ....

Interjections

𝕳𝔲𝔰𝔥 !

Interjections are words "thrown" into a sentence to express some sudden emotion or feeling, such as joy, sorrow, pain, triumph or surprise. An exclamation mark (!) is written after an interjection.

Examples: Hush! Hurrah! Oh! Alas!

A) Choose the most suitable interjection to fill the blank spaces in the following sentences.
(*Stop! Bravo! Open up! Alas! Hello! Oh! Hush! Good gracious! Halt! Shame on you! Help! Ouch! Hurrah!*)

the little girl is crying

1. .... ! who's speaking?
2. .... ! don't make a sound.
3. .... ! that hurts.
4. .... ! he died young.
5. .... ! we have won the cup.
6. .... ! what is that?
7. .... ! you pinched me.
8. .... ! man overboard.
9. .... ! who goes there.
10. .... ! he rescued the little girl.
11. .... ! police on duty.
12. .... ! road up.
13. .... ! the little girl is crying.

To exclaim means to cry out in anger, surprise, joy, sadness, pain, warning etc. and such exclamations should be followed by an exclamation mark.

Example: someone admiring a view might say: "What a marvellous sight this is!"

Note: an interjection need not necessarily be used with these exclamations.

B) Write the exclamations which the following people might make.

1. A captain urging on his team.
2. A person warning a child to keep away from something.
3. A huntsman who has spotted a fox.
4. An explorer on making a great discovery.
5. A person whose holiday has been spoiled by bad weather.
6. A player shouting to a team-mate on the football pitch.
7. A doctor warning a patient on the dangers of smoking.
8. A jockey speaking as he crosses the finishing line.
9. An angry policeman giving out to a careless motorist.

Creative Writing
A trip to the island

Write a imaginative essay about the day your uncle took you on a sailing trip to an island.

Helpful Ideas and Vocabulary

..... sunrise ..... silent harbour ..... uncle and cousins ..... waiting ..... untied mooring rope ..... hoisted sails ..... out into the wide bay ..... fresh breeze ..... slicing through the water ..... fishing ..... a dozen mackerel ..... the island on the horizon .....

..... rudder ..... steering the boat towards ..... eager to land ..... small sandy beach ..... hauled up boat ..... collected driftwood ..... lit campfire ..... cooked a delicious meal ..... appetites satisfied ..... thirst quenched .....

explored island ..... stone walls ..... meadows ..... bright flowers ..... rabbit warrens ..... climbed a rocky headland ..... came upon an ancient fort ..... sheer cliff ..... pounding waves below ..... wheeling gulls ..... time to return ..... packed ..... sailing swiftly homewards .....

Creative Writing

A jungle adventure

Helpful Ideas and Vocabulary

.. hardy pack-animals ..... hot and humid (damp) ..... tangled vegetation ..... hacked away
riously ..... dense canopy of foliage (leaves) ..... dark and sinister ..... swarming flies .....
ming beetles ..... gloriously coloured butterflies ..... chattering monkeys ..... whistling and
reeching ..... twittering and chirping of birds ..... majestic eagle soaring .....

eep into the rain forest ..... treacherous quicksand ..... gigantic snakes ..... the prowling jaguar
... king of the jungle ..... trudged onwards ..... encountered hostile Indians ..... outnumbered
nd surrounded ..... mortal danger ..... bargained for our freedom ..... departed hastily.

... advanced steadily ..... an immense river ..... Amazon ..... paddled canoes ..... swift current
... dangerous rapids ..... escaped unscathed (without injury) .....

Grammatical errors

Correct one error in each of the following sentences.

1. "You acted wrong," said his mother.
2. he got a lend of my new bicycle.
3. Shakespeare wrote the play "hamlet".
4. Christine is the tallest of the two girls.
5. More than one person were involved in the production.
6. At half past eight the procession past our door.
7. Neither Pat or Mary are going to the concert tonight.
8. The actor played the principal roll in the play.
9. My mother thought the doll was to expensive.
10. Many of the wounded men died from thirst in the desert.
11. She choose a book from the shelf and read the title.
12. Whos the lady whose sister was killed in the accident?
13. The twins shared the bunch of grapes between the players.
14. Sarah lives in No. 9 Cherry Avenue.
15. He is the eldest inhabitant in the town.
16. A native of Scotland is called a scotsman.
17. I bought a history novel in the book shop.
18. In winter they never go nowhere.
19. Stephen's painting was very different to that of his sister's.
20. It's a pity its snowing in the country.
21. The children had no school either on Saturday nor on Sunday.
22. Each of the girls have a room in the hotel.
23. "This antique is most unique," commented the expert.
24. He knew that the strange bird was a owl.
25. The cunning fox ran of with a plump chicken.
26. The boy had rang the bell without first looking at the name on the door.
27. She should have went to visit her grandmother yesterday.
28. You and me were very lucky to escape from the fire.
29. Tom or Kathleen must have took the pen.
30. Who did you see at the dance last night?
31. Ursula is the smallest of the two girls.
32. Pat and her ran awway from the vicious dog.
33. The king did not know who had did the evil act.
34. He taught he had made a big mistake.
35. The artist's work is much superior than mine.
36. It was not him who robbed the bank.
37. Everybody must bring their tennis racket.
38. This is the robin who built its nest in our garage.
39. Either the king or the queen are going to present the award.
40. They made quiet a considerable commotion.

Christine is the tallest of the two girls.

Descriptive Sounds

the babble of a stream
the murmur of a stream
the bang of a drum
the blare of a trumpet
the booming of a gun
the ring of a telephone
the call of a bugle
the chug of an engine
the clanking of chains
the clatter of hoofs
the clink of coins
the crackling of wood
the crack of a whip
the creak of a hinge
the dripping of water
the howling of the wind
the patter of feet
the patter of rain
the pealing of bells
the purr of an engine
the whirring of wings
the tinkle of glass
the swish of skirts
the rustling of silk (leaves)
the wail of the siren
the popping of corks
the rumble of a train

Crowds

a huge crowd
a great multitude
a mass of people
thronged with....
crowded with....
black with....
swarming with....
teeming with....
dotted with....
a street mob
a church congregation
football spectators
a concert audience

Useful Adjectives

long, short;   first, last;
present, absent;   new, old;
fast, slow;   warm, cold;
high, low;   wide, narrow;
round, square;   deep, shallow;
hard, soft;   heavy, light;
full, empty;   bitter, sweet;
sharp, dull;   thick, thin;
clean, dirty;   pretty, ugly;
kind, cruel;   quiet, noisy;
intelligent, stupid;   gay, sad;
brave, cowardly;   proud, humble;

Useful Adverbs

quickly, slowly;   happily, sadly;
cruelly, gently;   wisely, foolishly;
richly, poorly;   bitterly, sweetly;
loudly, quietly;   rapidly, slowly;
seriously, light-heartedly;
intelligently, stupidly;
recklessly, carefully;
patiently, impatiently;
awkwardly, carefully;

Proverbs

Let sleeping dogs lie.
Every cloud has a silver lining.
A good beginning is half the battle.
A stitch in time saves nine.
Every dog has its day.
Better late than never.
Out of sight out of mind.
Birds of a feather flock together.
When in Rome do as the Romans.
To kill two birds with the one stone.
Practice makes perfect.
No news is good news.
A rolling stone gathers no moss.
Don't count your chickens before they are hatched.
The early bird catches the worm.
One swallow does not make a summer.

Similes

as sly as a fox
as tender as a chicken
as slow as a tortoise
as slow as a snail
as meek as a lamb
as brave as a lion
as proud as a peacock
as busy as a bee
as busy as an ant
as blind as a bat
as playful as a kitten
as red as a turkey cock
as fat as a pig
as strong as a horse
as strong as an ox
as happy as a lark
as mad as a March hare
as wise as an owl
as swift as a deer
as gentle as a lamb
as frisky as a lamb
as fierce as a lion
as slippery as an eel
as agile as a monkey
as hungry as a wolf
as graceful as a swan
as obstinate as a mule
as stubborn as a mule
as timid as a rabbit
as hairy as a gorilla
as sure-footed as a goat
as silly as a sheep
as fast as a hare
as brown as a berry
as sweet as honey
as white as snow
as fresh as a daisy
as purple as the heather
as green as grass
as sturdy as an oak
as cold as ice

as fat as a pig

as graceful as a swan

Collective Words

a brood of chickens
a gaggle of geese
a flock of geese
a paddling of ducks
a herd of cattle
a herd of antelope
a flock of birds
a flock of sheep
a swarm of bees
a swarm of insects
a hive of bees
a team of horses
a string of horses
a team of oxen
a pride of lions
a troop of monkeys
a herd of buffaloes
a nest of rabbits
a nest of mice
a pack of hounds
a pack of wolves
a down of hares
a fall of woodcock
a plague of locusts
a kennel of dogs
a herd of elephants
a wisp of snipe
a flight of doves
a plague of insects
a shoal of herring
a school of whales
a tribe of goats
a sloth of bears
a skulk of foxes
a pride of lions
a flight of swallows
a barren of mules
a covey of grouse
a litter of pups
a litter of cubs

94

Masculine and Feminine of Nouns

prince	princess	giant	giantess
king	queen	brave	squaw
earl	countess	mayor	mayoress
emperor	empress	instructor	instructress
host	hostess	grandfather	grandmother
duke	duchess	manservant	maidservant
count	countess	postman	postwoman
baron	baroness	author	authoress
peer	peeress	heir	heiress
prophet	prophetess	traitor	traitress
wizard	witch	enchanter	enchantress
father	mother	deacon	deaconess
hero	heroine	beau	belle
husband	wife	shepherd	shepherdess
lad	lass	tailor	tailoress
gentleman	lady	warder	wardress
brother	sister		
tutor	governess	**Animals**	
lord	lady	colt	filly
master	mistress	buck rabbit	doe rabbit
nephew	niece	bull	cow
son	daughter	jack ass	jenny ass
sir	madam	gander	goose
man	woman	steer	heifer
landlord	landlady	dog	bitch
headmaster	headmistress	boar	sow
bridegroom	bride	cock	hen
bachelor	spinster	stag	hind
widower	widow	fox	vixen
actor	actress	ram	ewe
abbot	abbess	billy goat	nanny goat
monk	nun	cock sparrow	hen sparrow
priest	priestess	bullock	heifer
waiter	waitress	tiger	tigress
manager	manageress	lion	lioness
negro	negress	bull seal	cow seal
poet	poetess	leopard	leopardess
god	goddess	tom cat	tabby cat
step-father	step-mother	he-wolf	she-wolf
steward	stewardess	drake	duck
		stallion	mare

Words often confused

accept	dual		
except	duel		
adapt	emigrant		
adopt	immigrant		
allowed	faint		
aloud	feint		
bare	hanged		
bear	hung		
beside	hoard		
besides	horde		
board	human		
bored	humane		
brake	idle		
break	idol		
check	into		
cheque	in to		
coarse	lead		
course	led		
compare	loose		
contrast	lose		
council	peace		
counsel	piece		
current	persecute		
currant	prosecute		
decease	plain		
disease	plane		
desert	pray		
dessert	prey		
discover	sight		
invent	site		

Words often misspelt

across	heaven
address	height
already	heroes
altogether	humour
amount	jealous
arctic	jewellery
argument	lightning
author	marriage
balloon	meant
beautiful	medicine
believe	minute
careful	naive
chaos	necessary
chief	nuisance
circuit	offered
college	ordinary
colonel	paid
conceive	pigeon
despair	privilege
develop	professor
dying	prove
difference	queue
disappear	really
excellent	receive
excitement	referee
family	restaurant
fiery	seize
forty	sentence
friend	skilful
guard	